More GREAT SOUTHERN MYSTERIES

More GREAT SOUTHERN MYSTERIES

Florida's Fountain of Youth, Ghosts of the Alamo,
Lost Maidens of the Okefenokee, Terror on the Natchez Trace
and other Enduring Mysteries of the American South

E. RANDALL FLOYD

Author of GREAT SOUTHERN MYSTERIES

August House Publishers, Inc.

LITTLE ROCK

Printed in the United States of America

10 9 8 7 6 5 4 3 2 1

LIBRARY OF CONGRESS CATALOGING-IN-PUBLICATION DATA

More Great Southern Mysteries / [collected by] E. Randall Floyd—
1st ed.
p.   cm.
Includes bibliographical references (p. 187)
ISBN 0-87483-160-1 (HB : acid-free) : $16.95
1. Southern States—History, Local. 2. Curiosities and wonders—
Southern States. 3. Legends—Southern States.
I. Floyd, E. Randall.
F209.5M67 1990
975—dc20   90-1194

First Edition, 1990

Executive: Liz Parkhurst
Project editor: Judith Faust
Design director: Ted Parkhurst
Cover illustration: Byron Taylor
Typography: Lettergraphics, Little Rock

This book is printed on archival-quality paper which meets the
guidelines for performance and durability of the Committee on
Production Guidelines for Book Longevity of the
Council on Library Resources.

AUGUST HOUSE, INC.   PUBLISHERS   LITTLE ROCK

*This book is
dedicated to
Anne*

Preface

After the publication of my first book, *Great Southern Mysteries,* a lot of people wanted to know two things—where did I get all my story ideas, and why on earth was I so attracted to unexplained mysteries?

The first question was easy enough to answer—I spend a lot of time at the public library, as well as in my personal library at home. At one point I figured my wife and I owned close to five thousand books and subscribed to dozens of newspapers, magazines, and professional periodicals.

The second question, however, was a little harder to deal with. For starters, I haven't the faintest clue why I am so drawn to stories dealing with the unexplained, the bizarre, the paranormal. Could be that I just love a good shudder every now and then, but I suspect it's something deeper.

All of us are fascinated by the Unknown. If you don't believe that, just look at the list of titles at the corner bookstore or check out the local movie marquee. Demons, ghosts, time travel, witches, and ungodly creatures straight out of Lovecraft seem to dominate our popular culture.

But this is nothing new. Down through the ages, men and women have tingled and shivered at things they couldn't understand—the strange sound at the window late at night, an unexplained presence flitting across the moonlit lawn, a stranger on the subway who stares oddly out at the world.

These fears, both real and imaginary, are certainly holdovers from another era in our evolutionary development. They go back to a time perhaps when every creaking thing in nature had its own sinister purpose—the sun, the rain, the wind, the moon, the shadows, the forest.

In classical times, there were horned cyclops and winged monsters that terrorized lonely islands far out at sea. During the middle ages, the trackless forests of Europe were haunted by witches and goblins and dragons that only sainted heroes could eradicate. Recently, new horrors have been unleashed upon the world—nuclear weapons, global warming, and AIDS, to name a few.

These new horrors, threatening as they are, pale when compared to the vampires and werewolves and other blood-sucking nightmares of lore. At least we can understand the effects of fallout and the consequences of the AIDS virus. We can protect ourselves, if we try, against those "mysteries"— but how can you tell a couple of Boy Scouts huddled around a campfire in a lonely swamp that the snapping sounds they hear off in the distance are just the wind rustling in the trees? How do you protect a child from the lurking shadows in an open closet?

Some mysteries are less terrifying than they are just plain baffling. When someone suddenly disappears in full view of onlookers, when eerie blue lights dance and hover over a misty cemetery, when a tribe of beautiful young women are discovered in the middle of the Okefenokee Swamp, or when a pair of human footprints are found in stone too many millions of years old, you start to worry about the "natural" order of things.

The Deep South, probably more than any other region of the country, remains shrouded in mystery and legend. This book is about some of those mysteries and legends, told from the viewpoint of an inquiring journalist.

Obviously a few of the narratives contained herein border on the fanciful. But, lest we forget, a wise man once said that behind every legend there is a least a grain of truth. And I say that behind every mystery, there is the possibility of some new scientific discovery.

Whether you accept what you read in this book as fact or fiction isn't really important. The main thing is that by reading it, you're helping keep alive some of the wondrous mysteries of our region's fascinating past.

I couldn't have gotten away with this book without the warm, and often splendid, cooperation of my wife, Anne—a generous and caring companion with an editor's soul. Also, this project was made easier by the chairman of the history department where I work, Dr. Ed Cashin, whose inspiration and wise comments were helpful in tracking down certain bits of renegade information.

I'd like to certainly thank my editors at August House, especially Judith Faust, for their valuable advice and instructive criticism of the original manuscript.

Lastly, there is no way that this or any of my other editorial projects could have become a reality without the input of my late uncle, the Rev. Henry Curtiss Tillman, a master storyteller and writer. I'm sure that somewhere up there Uncle Curt is curled up in a quiet corner with a book—hopefully one of mine.

E. Randall Floyd
Augusta, Georgia
1990

Contents

Secrets from Beyond the Grave

Gold, Shrines, and Ancient Stones

Improbable Encounters

Encounters With the Unknown

Lost Causes and Blood-stained Myths

Demons And Delusions

*Entertaining Satan
in the Old Dominion*

When most Americans think of witches and witchcraft, they usually think of the hysteria that swept through the tiny village of Salem, Massachusetts, near the end of the seventeenth century.

By the time the persecutions were over, scores of innocent citizens—mostly old, impoverished women—had been beaten, stoned, and tortured for practicing what the state called "diabolical black arts." They were the lucky ones. At least twenty poor souls either went to the gallows or were crushed to death beneath heavy stones for dabbling in that most heinous of crimes, witchcraft.

The Salem witch trials may have made history, but the first documented case of witchcraft in the United States involving a white woman occurred almost seven decades earlier in Virginia.

In 1626, Goodwife Joan Wright, an upstanding resident of Surrey County, across the river from Jamestown, was accused by a number of neighbors of having "consorted with the devil." The exact circumstances surrounding her crimes were never fully revealed, but accusations ranged from having put a spell on chickens to having made young women "dance naked and stand before the Tree." The "Tree" was a reference to Satan's own special tree, around which young maidens anxious to join a coven were required to dance and "perform other lewd acts unfitting to Nature."

Mrs. Wright was eventually acquitted of the charges, but there would be other cases in the coming years. In all cases, though, punishment was generally light compared to the harsh sentences handed down by the notorious "Witch Courts" of Salem, Boston, and elsewhere in New England. At least no one in Virginia was ever tortured or hanged for practicing witchcraft.

Almost all seventeenth century English men and women believed in Satan and the witches and sorcerers who served him. In 1597 King James had published his famous *Daemonologie,* a frightfully medieval epistle which set forth the monarch's own verifications for the existence of the devil and his unholy hosts. According to James, the only way to deal effectively with these agents of the Prince of Darkness was to seek them out and destroy them wherever they may have been hiding.

When the English settlers first arrived in the New World, their suspicions about devils were confirmed. Everywhere they looked they saw devils—in the dark forests, among the remote mountain tops, and along the streams and rivers that flowed through their wild, new homeland. These "devils" were the Indians, of course: dark-skinned, half-naked, unfathomable savages whose bizarre rituals and bloodthirsty ceremonies terrified the European newcomers.

Commenting on the Indians, Captain John Smith once declared that they had "entertained him with most strange and fearful Conjurations."

Soon, however, as more settlers arrived and the Indians were pushed back deeper into the forests, the emphasis on the "black devils" shifted to "white devils" among the English colonists themselves. When Goodwife Wright was discovered engaging in witchcraft, colonial authorities moved swiftly to uncover others in her coven.

The best known case of witchcraft in the southern colonies involved another Virginia woman, named Grace Sherwood. By all accounts Mrs. Sherwood was a popular and well-liked citizen of Lynnhaven Bay, a sparsely settled community on the southern shores of Chesapeake Bay. Why she was accused of witchcraft in the first place remains a mystery. She was certainly no crone. No black cats followed her around, and no bats had been seen swooping around her eaves late at night. She also happened to be married to one of the community's most upstanding businessmen.

Sherwood's arrest and later ordeal in a "ducking pond" probably had something to do with blight suddenly appearing on a neighbor's crop. Then, too, the same neighbor's pigs suddenly started behaving queerly—always a good sign that unnatural forces were at work nearby. To many folks in the community, it seemed unlikely so many unfortunate events could happen to one family so quickly without some kind of "outside" interference.

There could only be one explanation—witchcraft. The finger of suspicion pointed directly at Sherwood when yet another neighbor testified she had been "ridden about" by Grace Sherwood and that the suspect had left her house once "out of the Key hole...like a black Catt."

Proclaiming her innocence, Mrs. Sherwood was bound over to the General Court in Williamsburg to stand trial. The charge: consorting with the devil and engaging in witchcraft. The judge quickly ruled that the evidence was "too general" and remanded the case to the county.

Back at Lynnhaven Bay, it was decided that the only way to determine Sherwood's guilt or innocence was to administer to her the water test. In those days, it was widely believed that water was the purest element in nature. It stood to reason, then, that diabolical creatures like witches and demons would never be accepted by water. In other words, guilty persons would float on the surface, while innocent ones would sink to the bottom.

The problem was, should the accused person happen to be innocent, there was a good chance he or she would drown. On the other hand, should the unfortunate individual's clothing somehow trap a pocket of air and cause him or her to float, it would be an indisputable sign of guilt. The gallows awaited those who floated.

On the fateful day—July 10, 1706—Grace Sherwood was

bound and gagged, and then hauled down to a spot on the bay known as Witch Duck Point. When the charges had been properly read once more and the Christian rites administered, she was rowed out on the water, prayed for, then dumped overboard.

For several seconds her prosecutors listened to her strangled cries, and then felt a sense of relief when her thrashing body finally sank beneath the rippling waves. Spectators lined along the shore dropped to their knees and prayed for the witch's soul.

Suddenly, out of nowhere, a mass of angry black clouds began forming overhead. Thunder boomed and lightning clawed across the troubled heavens. The rain came, drenching the crowds of God-fearing colonists assembled on the muddy shore. Those who were there later described it as a deluge, as if God Himself had opened up the gates to paradise to let loose His terrible wrath.

Then, out on the water, the impossible happened—the soggy form of Grace Sherwood was rising slowly from the murky depths of the bay.

She was floating!

The terrified prosecutors in the boat didn't know whether to fish her out of the water or to row away from that accursed place as fast as they could. They finally decided they'd seen enough miracles for one day. Guilty or not, they simply couldn't let the poor woman drown, so they hauled her into the boat and rowed back to the beach.

There still had to be a trial, of course, and Mrs. Sherwood was eventually found guilty. But several months later, about the time the Salem witch trials were winding down, Grace Sherwood was released.

She had been one of the lucky ones. In spite of her trials and tribulations as a witch suspect, she lived to the ripe old age of eighty—unlike some of the less fortunate women in Salem Village.

The Sacred
"Woman in Blue"

When Spanish missionaries reached the Texas wilderness in the early 1600s, they heard a lot of strange stories from local Indians about mysterious, white-skinned gods who had once walked among them.

According to some accounts, these divine visitors had spoken to them in a language different from theirs, but one they could understand. Most of these gods had come and gone in ages past, but all held forth a common promise—they would come again someday.

The story that got the most attention concerned a beautiful young white "goddess" who, legend has it, appeared among several groups of Indians living in Texas and elsewhere in the Southwest. The Indians called her the "woman in blue" because each time she came she wore a blue cloak—similar, in fact, to those worn by the newly arrived Spanish priests.

Not only was this "woman in blue" a frequent visitor, she was said to have left behind material evidence of her earthly visits—including a portable stone altar adorned with religious emblems and the figures of several saints. There was even a figure of Christ himself!

Intrigued by such stories, missionary leaders wasted no time informing the church back in Spain about their findings. This seemed to be a mystery of profound spiritual significance—how was it that pagan savages living on the far edge of this strange, wild New World had come into possession of the very symbols of Christian faith?

Within a short while, droves of other missionaries, accompanied by soldiers and explorers, flocked to Texas. Their task: solve the mystery of the "woman in blue."

One of the missionaries who came was Father Damien Manzanet, who had recently read a new book entitled *The Mystical City of God*. In the book, Sister Maria de Agreda, a Castilian nun, had told how she had been mysteriously transported to a remote wilderness on the frontiers of New Spain, where she had introduced a heathen race to Christianity.

Sister Maria, a respected abbess who had entered the monastery at the age of fifteen, claimed to have made the mystical journey more than five hundred times in the early seventeenth century. In glowing words she related how she had been well received by dark-skinned savages who called themselves "Titlas," or "Tejas," and that they had miraculously understood her every word.

Maria's out-of-body travels apparently occurred only when she slept. Without being too specific, the sister said she would suddenly grow rigid in bed. A state of supreme ecstasy would seize her, and she would be whisked away at blinding speed to the wilderness where she worked and prayed among naked savages.

By 1630 all of Spain was abuzz with talk of Sister Maria's "holy mystery." To make the story even more interesting, a group of fifty Jumano Indians had appeared at a convent in northeastern Mexico that same year, asking that missionaries be sent among them. When pressed to explain their sudden interest in European religion, the Indians said a graceful white woman—a "goddess"—had come to them long ago and instructed them in "the truths of Christian faith."

Who could that white "goddess" have been? Except for the wife or mistress of an occasional explorer or trader, there was no record of European women having visited that part of the New World. Even more perplexing were the religious artifacts apparently left behind by the "woman in blue."

The more Father Manzanet listened to the stories, the more convinced he became of a connection between Sister

Maria's account of her out-of-body travels and the tales told by these brooding savages on the frontier. In her book, she had called them Titlas. Is that not what these Indians he encountered called themselves—Titlas...Tejas...Techas?

The similarities were all the proof the Franciscan priest needed to convince himself that it was Maria de Agreda who had visited these Indians long ago. Just why, and when, he wasn't sure. But the bottom line was that God had used Sister Maria and her miracles to lead him to the wilderness, too.

Like most seventeenth century Spaniards, Father Manzanet believed strongly in supernatural forces, and that divine intervention was an everyday fact of life. Like most of his countrymen, he readily embraced the possibility that Maria de Agreda had been telling the truth when she wrote about her otherworldly travels—that God had indeed sent her among the Indians in the New World to preach and spread the Gospel.

It was Maria's story, in fact, that had spurred legions of missionaries across the Rio Grande into the Texas hinterlands. While some established missions and sought to convert Indians, many searched for proof of the holy sister's travels. As they pressed deeper into Texas, the missionaries heard other stories about the "blue lady." One chief said she had healed his mother by touching her brow. Another legend told how delicate blue flowers always blossomed wherever she stepped.

Father Manzanet himself was once asked by a withered old chief for a piece of blue cloth in which to bury his wife. The Father, stunned by the request, asked why it should be blue. "Because," said the chief, "that was the color of the cloak worn long ago by the beautiful young woman who had come to Texas to tell us about God."

The story of the "woman in blue" would be like a magnet in later decades, drawing hundreds of other missionaries and explorers to the Texas territory. Today the Southwest abounds with legends about the mysterious "goddess," who some believe still roams the hills and deserts causing flowers to bloom and bestowing love and riches on the unfortunate.

19

The Lost Maidens of the Okefenokee

Spanish explorers pushing northward through the gloomy Florida swamps into the moss-shrouded lowlands of Georgia were astonished to encounter tales about a mysterious race of women who supposedly lived somewhere in the Okefenokee, that dismal region the Indians called the "land of the trembling earth."

In pre-Colonial days, the Okefenokee was home to various groups of Indians, many of whom believed that devils and demons occupied the deeper recesses of the dreary swamp. Legends about witches and angry spirits also swirled around crackling campfires, and even into modern times, there were stories about a horrible, fire-breathing monster said to dwell in a bottomless lake somewhere far out in the middle of that shadow-haunted wilderness.

When the first conquistadors arrived in the early sixteenth century, they heard these stories and more. The tales that fascinated them the most, though, had to do with a tribe of beautiful, dark-eyed maidens known collectively as the "Daughters of the Sun."

It was said that these women, who "spoke in accents of music and had the countenance of angels," lived on an enchanted island called Lost Paradise far out in the middle of the Okefenokee. The island, so the story went, was hidden from view by swirling mists and protected by deep rivers and alligator-filled lakes. Lost Paradise was believed to have been the original Garden of Eden.

Unfortunately, the whereabouts of the island was a closely guarded secret. As with El Dorado—another fabled, much sought-after goal in the North American wilderness—only a few oldtimers had ever laid eyes upon either the enchanted land itself or the beautiful "Daughters of the Sun" who dwelled there.

One old story, handed down by generations of Indians and white settlers, referred to the island as a "magical realm" full of softly gurgling streams, game-filled forests, and air so clean and pure that flowers bloomed year-round. When the conquistadors first heard of the place, they began to fantasize about the lovely damsels. Weary from long months in the wilderness, these grim explorers in gleaming armor pressed their wary Indian hosts for more information.

Alas, the old Indian chiefs—even at sword-point—refused to reveal the location of Lost Paradise. Frustrated, the Spaniards set off in search of the women themselves. Some time later, exhausted and running low on supplies, the bearded conquistadors reluctantly abandoned their quest.

When other Europeans arrived in later years, they, too, heard fascinating accounts of the "Daughters of the Sun." As with their Spanish predecessors, all attempts to find them failed—sometimes tragically.

For example, Creek legend tells about a group of white hunters who became "dizzy" and "disoriented" while searching for the women. Soon they were overcome with fatigue and collapsed. Suddenly, out of the dreamlike mists, several of the most beautiful women they had ever seen appeared. Radiant in the early morning sun, these angelic apparitions reportedly took pity on the pale-skinned visitors and transported them to their enchanted island where they were nursed back to health.

As soon as they had recovered, the intruders were whisked away from Lost Paradise in a cloud of smoke. But the Europeans, smitten by the beauty of the maidens—and perhaps determined to make them their wives—trudged back into the swamp to find them. They never returned, and their fate remains a mystery in the folklore of the Okefenokee Swamp.

Another Creek legend deals with a similar incident, this one involving a couple of lost Indian braves. After days of wandering around the swamp, the hapless Indians stumbled upon a village populated by beautiful, dark-eyed women. These women had husbands, however, who were "fierce... and exceedingly cruel to strangers."

Convinced that the women were the legendary Daughters of the Sun, the braves decided to fight rather than be forced out of the enchanted forest by their husbands. The maidens, teary-eyed and full of great fear for the young intruders' lives, begged them to go before their husbands returned from a hunting trip. The braves obeyed, and upon returning to their village they recounted their adventures in the Okefenokee.

Soon other braves set out to find the enchanted island, but their efforts were all in vain. After years of searching the wild swamp, they finally gave up, convinced that neither the island nor the women had existed in the first place.

Still, over the years, other explorers pressing deep into the rugged interior of the Okefenokee heard soft laughter echoing through the dim glades. On more than one occasion, solitary adventurers told of having seen thin, shimmering forms flitting through the tangled shadows.

Who were the "lost maidens" of the Okefenokee? One theory holds that the mysterious women belonged to a long-forgotten group of Mayans who had migrated to the Okefenokee region from their homeland in Mexico a thousand years ago. Another says the maidens were descended from survivors of Atlantis, the legendary continent that was said to have sunk beneath the Atlantic Ocean in a cataclysmic upheaval in pre-Biblical times.

Whatever their origins—or whether in fact they ever existed at all—the legend of the Daughters of the Sun stands as one of the Okefenokee Swamp's most delightful and charming mysteries.

Visions of the Veil-Born

Once upon a time, long before interstate highways and jet travel, the lonely backroads of the Deep South were dangerous places for solitary wayfarers. Besides Indians, wild animals, and cold-blooded highwaymen, other terrors lurked among the remote hills and swamps—fanciful terrors that belong more in the realm of folklore than history.

To the people of that far-off age, creatures like *loups-garous,* wampus cats, and will-o-the-wisp hobgoblins were every bit as real as bloodthirsty Indians, masked desperados, and snarling bears.

Probably the most dreaded creature of them all was the "plat-eye," a much-feared, much-misunderstood spirit that haunted and tormented its victims unmercifully before driving them either to insane asylums or early graves. Many spine-tingling stories are told about bizarre encounters with this peculiar apparition, mainly among early settlers pushing westward through the Appalachian Mountains and farther south along the Mississippi Delta.

To meet up with this loathsome creature on a lonely road at night meant sure doom for unlucky travelers. That's why in the old days folks tried their best to avoid certain hollows, woods, and swamps when going cross-country. Even today, in some parts of the Great Smoky Mountains it is considered sheer folly to pass by a graveyard at night. The same is true among the lowlands of Mississippi, Florida, Georgia, Alabama, and Louisiana where the horrible plat-eye is known to still lurk.

But in the past, there must have been a lot of people who ignored this advice because folklore is riddled with hair-raising run-ins between hapless humans and these fearsome creatures of the dark.

According to legends probably brought over from Europe, plat-eyes were evil spirits that came back to life for one of several reasons—to avenge their deaths, to cause mischief among mortals, or to finish up tasks began in life. Failure to provide the departed with a proper burial was also a good way to warrant an unwelcome visit by the plat-eye.

The biggest problem about plat-eyes, however, was that they were invisible to most people. Only a few special persons, usually young girls, had the power to see these wispy shades. In some regions of the South, these individuals were known as the "veil-born" because of having been born with a caul—a thin membrane, similar to that inside an egg shell, which surrounds a fetus. A few babies are born with the membrane enveloping their heads.

Stories about the veil-born and their mystical powers are still commonplace, especially among rural blacks who believe that children born with cauls have the gift of second sight—the ability to see things invisible to most people. Ghosts, goblins, and plat-eyes are among the spooks said to inhabit this unseen world. In medieval Europe, persons born with cauls were often persecuted as witches.

In time, stories about the plat-eye joined those of other fabulous creatures said to haunt the American frontier. The wampus cat, *loup-garou,* and even Bigfoot seem closely related to the plat-eye myth and may share similar origins.

When black slaves arrived from Africa in the early seventeenth century, they brought with them their own pantheon of gods, demons, and an assortment of other spiritual entities. These victims of the "peculiar institution" may have actually been the first to introduce the plat-eye myth. At least, they gave it new terrifying substance. Like their African ancestors, slaves believed that to bury a person without proper funeral rites was the fastest way to get an angry visit from the deceased's ghost. To die without benefit of a funeral meant the dead person was cursed to wander the face of the earth forever—or until it could be banished through exorcism.

In African mythology, funerals were essential in helping the dead find the right road to heaven and bypass the less desirable pathway to hell. In the absence of such rites, the ghost would be condemned to the unpleasant task of haunting houses and cemeteries and out-of-the-way roads. Without graveside ceremonies such as feasting, prayer, singing, and the cleansing of the body, these spirits would sometimes be compelled, zombie-like, to go after their relatives with a bloodthirsty vengeance.

As a rule, plat-eye spirits generally resemble the bodies they once occupied, but they also take different shapes—sometimes a dog or cat, other times a pig or cow, or even another human being without a head. Plat-eyes have no natural enemies and will stop at nothing to terrorize a particular place—such as a house, forest, or graveyard—until proper funeral arrangements are made. That's why such places—especially graveyards—are to be avoided.

"The vicinity of cemeteries is carefully avoided after dark," wrote one observer, "and so are places where people have met with fatal misfortune."

The Bell Witch of Tennessee

When John Bell first heard the horrible scratching sound at the walls of his remote Tennessee homestead, he thought it was rats trying to gnaw their way in out of the winter cold.

Several nights in a row he had set traps, but nothing seemed to work against the pesky rodents. The sounds continued, night after night—the scratching and clawing and hissing—keeping his family up until all hours. The strange thing was that no matter how hard he looked, he never saw the first sign of a rat.

Then came a new sound, tappings at the window, soon followed by a mysterious scratching at the door—like a wild animal trying to get in. Most chilling of all, however, were the eerie cries that seemed to float down the chimney long after the fire had gone out at night.

Bell was not a superstitious man. All his life he had believed there was an answer to every mystery, no matter how puzzling. That's why it took him so long to come to the conclusion that the strange noises were being made by a ghost or spirit or some such supernatural thing.

In those days—back in the early 1800s—much of Tennessee was wild and remote, full of old stories and legends about "spirits of the earth." These spirits were said to be mostly benign—actually helpful to the hard-working pioneers of the lonely forests and mountains. But occasionally tales cropped up about less friendly ones, malign spirits that sought to harm and destroy rather than help and instruct.

When neighbors heard about the strange goings-on out at

the Bell place, they figured something evil had to be behind the commotion. What they couldn't figure out was why.

"If we didn't know them (the Bells) for the good and honest people that they were," one neighbor reported in a local newspaper, "we'd have thought they were being punished for some crime or sin they'd committed."

By the winter of 1818, life at the Bell farm had become so bizarre Bell thought seriously about moving his family away. Pictures would fall mysteriously off walls; tables would turn on their sides and scuttle across the kitchen floor; chairs would prance about, and once even did a few somersaults; cutlery would parade up and down on the floor; china dishes and cups would "march merrily along" the tables and cabinets.

Before long, accounts of the eerie happenings began to appear in newspapers as far away as New York and Philadelphia. Reporters, ministers, doctors and psychic researchers soon descended on the Bell household along with hundreds of curiosity seekers. The Bell farm had become what one reporter called "a place of occult pilgrimage...."

The presence of so many visitors actually seemed to encourage the spooky antics at the old Bell place. Whenever outsiders called upon the "spirit" to do something, it always obliged, sometimes making vague whispering sounds and indistinct mutterings while whipping sheets and quilts through the air and causing the clock to chime for hours at a time.

"As an entertainment," declared one visitor, "it was in a class of its own. Put it in New York, set it on Broadway, and you could sell tickets from now till kingdom come."

A journalist writing in a Baltimore newspaper said, "It was as if the thing knew what was expected of it and was determined that no one who traveled there would be disappointed. It obligingly put on its act even without being asked to—and, if you did speak to it, it would mostly do whatever was requested."

On March 14, 1818, the first distinguishable words came forth from the spirit. In the presence of several astonished visitors and the entire Bell family, a crackling woman's voice said: "I am a spirit who was once happy...but now I have been disturbed and am unhappy."

The spirit identified herself simply as "Kate." She said she was now a witch of the forest, but had once lived as a woman on the land "long, long ago." Kate informed her listeners that she was haunting the Bell farm because someone had disturbed her bones. "My bones were buried near here," Kate stated matter-of-factly, "and I want them back."

Although Mr. Bell succeeded in finding what he believed were the old woman's bones and providing them with a proper Christian burial, the annoying spirit refused to leave them alone. In fact, Bell's noble action seemed only to make matters worse—especially for Bell himself, who thereafter became the favorite target of the old spirit's mischievous antics.

First of all, the victimized farmer's tongue began to swell until it filled most of his mouth. He could hardly eat, speak, or even swallow water. His physical condition quickly deteriorated as the old witch tormented him.

"We have seen nothing like it in our experience of morbid and pathological conditions," one attending physician was quoted in a local paper as having uttered. "There appears to be no known reason for the affliction and there is certainly no known cure. We shall just have to hope, and to pray, that the patient makes a natural recovery."

Bell didn't recover. Instead, he grew steadily worse, as unseen hands reportedly slapped him sharply across the face, ripped clothes from his body, punched him in the stomach, and kicked him in the legs. On one occasion the witch even spat in his face.

"I've almost done with you, Jack Bell," the witch proclaimed. "It won't be long now before you go to your grave to rot!"

Investigators, neighbors, and members of Bell's family begged the old spirit to release the farmer from her wrath. "Why do you hate John Bell so?" Bell's best friend, Jack Johnson asked. "What has he ever done to harm or pester you? Won't you be courteous enough to answer my question?"

To this the witch replied: "I am a spirit from everywhere—from Heaven, Hell, and the Earth. I am in the air, in houses, anyplace at any time. I was born millions of years ago. That's all I have to say to you!"

So she continued to plague Bell and other members of the family, striking them with boils, colds, fevers, and the like. Betsy, Bell's teenage daughter, seemed to be the only one immune to the witch's spell.

Finally, on the morning of December 19, 1820, the farmer went into a stupor. His doctor said: "I can find nothing fatally wrong with him. Yet he is most assuredly dying."

The next day the doctor's words were proven. Bell's frail, tormented body was laid to rest in a tiny cemetery not far from the house where he had suffered for the better part of the past four years. At the funeral, the voice of the Bell witch was heard one last time, cackling and croaking triumphantly over the farmer's death. And then—just as mysteriously as it had appeared—it was gone forever.

Psychic investigators and journalists still write and talk about the Bell Witch haunting as if it had occurred only yesterday instead of nearly one hundred seventy years ago. So far, no satisfactory theory has come forth to account for the incredible events that entertained a generation of Americans and drove one Tennessee farmer to his grave.

Notorious Deeds
and Unnatural Acts

The Prophet's Bloody Revenge

On the morning of May 12, 1828, a young black slave and self-appointed preacher named Nat Turner was picking corn in his master's garden when a voice "like the sound of many winds" floated down to him from Heaven.

Turner, a short, powerfully built 28-year-old with clear, twinkly eyes, wasn't afraid. Nor was he really surprised as the voice whispered his name over and over, reminding him of his special purpose in life.

In fact, the soft-spoken slave had been expecting a miracle such as this for some time. Convinced since childhood that he was a prophet sent to earth on a divine mission, young Turner's eyes flashed with proud fire as he pondered the implications of that mystical vision.

There had been signs, even before God's voice came to him in the field that morning—disturbing signs that only Turner, the Almighty's Chosen One on earth, could interpret. Had he not seen in his own mind rivers of blood pouring throughout the land? Had he not heard thunder rolling through the heavens while others slept, warning of the coming clash between good and evil? Had he himself not witnessed an army of black and white angels waging spiritual warfare in the storm-scented clouds?

What were the strange lights in the sky he had watched flickering over the hilltops on several occasions if not the Saviour's own redeeming glow?

That morning, standing alone in the sweeping field of corn, had not the prophet seen drops of blood staining the cornstalks? And on the leaves of bushes, had he not seen the marks of Satan—strange numbers and hieroglyphs and a blasphemous parade of stick-like men reveling in gruesome poses?

With his face uplifted toward Heaven, young Nat Turner knew he had seen and heard all those things and more. He also knew it was only a matter of time before God's mighty sword slashed down, smiting the Serpent and all the enemies of His Chosen People.

Three years later, on a warm, summer evening in 1831, Nat Turner's mystical vision would come to pass. It would come only a few months after darkness engulfed the sun in a solar eclipse—the final sign the prophet needed before springing into action.

Cross Keys, Virginia, was a quiet hamlet nestled in the rolling hills of Southampton County in the southwestern corner of the state. In those days, Cross Keys was populated primarily by white farmers and merchants of modest means. One of the community's most prosperous residents was a kind, gentle farmer named Joseph Travis, who happened to own several slaves.

One of those slaves was Nat Turner.

Travis was fond of his young slave, admiring him not only for his intelligence and enthusiasm for work, but also for his honesty, courage, and religious piety. He had even attended a few of Turner's sermons and, according to some records, encouraged the preacher to continue developing his oratorical talents.

What Travis didn't know—nor did any other white person living in Southampton County that unusually warm, muggy summer in 1831—was that the black preacher he had come so to admire was secretly plotting one of the bloodiest slave insurrections in American history. By the time it ended, less than a month later, at least sixty white people would be dead along with more than a hundred blacks.

It is no secret that Turner, who openly called himself "The Prophet," had a mystical, almost mesmerizing influence over many people in the area, white as well as black. He was convinced of his own superiority, divinely granted by long hours of prayer and fasting in the name of Jehovah, the god of the Old Testament.

Therefore, when the time came to act, Turner had little trouble convincing a few fellow slaves that they, too, were part of his divine mission to rid the valley of whites. He told them all about his visions, about how God had spoken to him on numerous occasions, about the lights flashing over the hilltops, and the blood-stained cornstalks, all in preparation for him to lead the glorious task that lay ahead.

In his own chilling words, Turner later wrote: "I now began to prepare them too for my purpose by telling them something was about to happen that would terminate in fulfilling the great promise that had been made to me."

That "great promise" was death. It came quickly and mercilessly to the simple farmers and planters and tradesmen of Southampton County who lay sleeping in their beds when The Prophet and his axe-wielding band of "angels" struck.

The first white people to die were Turner's own master, Joseph Travis. and his entire family—hacked to death with axes. From the Travis farm a group of about thirty blacks armed with old muskets, knives, picks, and axes, surged across the countryside, stopping off at every house and cabin along the way to stab, beat, and shoot their white occupants to death.

The bloodiest carnage occurred at dawn the next morning when Turner's gang of killers broke into the home of a widow getting her ten children off to school. The mother and nine of her children were slaughtered on the spot; the tenth child escaped by crawling inside a chimney where she hid until the murderers went away.

By eight o'clock, the enraged black rebels had hacked and bludgeoned their way halfway across the county toward the tiny town of Jerusalem. When the alarm finally sounded— sometime around nine—hundreds of white men came charging after the renegade slaves, rifles and pistols blazing. Several blacks were killed outright; others, including Nat Turner, escaped into the Great Dismal Swamp.

Almost a month later, The Prophet was seen hiding in some bushes and apprehended by a team of marshals. On November 5 he was tried, found guilty, and sentenced to be hanged six days later on November 11. Throughout the ordeal—capture, trial and gallows—Turner remained calm and collected, seemingly unfazed by the angry demands for his life that swirled across the jailhouse lawn. Some say the divine mystic and rebel leader actually looked forward to his date with the hangman.

A few days before his scheduled execution, Turner set forth his thoughts and feelings about the grisly deed he had done. What emerged from his "confessions" was a rambling, sometimes incoherent outpouring of love for his fellow man. Nowhere, however, did there appear to be any signs of remorse for the tragic loss of life he had caused.

Yet Turner's confessions, shrouded in mysticism and religious symbolism, revealed the inner workings of a brilliant but deeply troubled young mind, consumed with burning visions and other Old Testament revelations about his divinely inspired mission—that of rising up against the whites and smiting them dead for having caused his people so much misery and suffering.

Commenting on his vision in the cornfield, Turner wrote, "I heard a loud noise in the Heavens, and the spirit instantly appeared to me and said the Serpent was loosened…and that I should…fight against the Serpent, for the time was fast approaching when the first would be last and the last should be first…."

Moments before the noose was placed over his neck, someone asked Turner whether he regretted what he had done. In a soft voice that crackled, the Prophet replied, "Was not Christ crucified?"

Virginia's "Starving Time"

Their small village wasn't much—a handful of crude huts and cabins surrounded by a hastily erected palisade to keep out wild animals and even wilder savages—but to the few hundred brave souls clustered along the lonely shore of Virginia, it was home.

In spite of the hardships and loneliness and unending peril that lurked just beyond the protective wall, these Jamestown colonists were determined to make a stand. No one thought about going back home to England. They were here, and here they would stay to build a new way of life—far removed from the dark, troubled ways of old Europe.

This was not the first time, of course, that a small band of English colonists had tried to make a go of it in the harsh western wilderness. Only a few years before, in 1587, more than a hundred men, women, and children had apparently been wiped out by Indians in an ill-fated attempt to colonize a small island named Roanoke off the Virginia coast. Then, just three years past, another group of settlers had set up camp at the mouth of the Sagadahoc River in Maine. Although not quite as disastrous as the Roanoke Colony, the Maine effort had also failed.

The most recent attempt at colonization had come less than two years earlier when seventy-five men and boys had tried to set up the Jamestown settlement for future waves of colonists. Instead of worrying about finding food, those first Englishmen in Jamestown had been more concerned about finding gold and an illusive passageway to China. Their foolhardiness cost most of them their lives.

The Jamestown of 1609 would be different. This time, instead of spending all their time and energy searching for nonexistent gold and the fabled passageway to the Far East, the colonists would clear the forests, raise crops, and become totally self-sufficient. Some five hundred men, women, and children had come along this time for the purpose of building new lives at the edge of this mythological, legend-haunted New World.

Then the first snowflakes of winter fell. As the days grew shorter and the nights darker and colder, some settlers began to realize there wasn't going to be enough food to go around. The crops had not matured as expected, and the water itself had become contaminated. To make matters worse, no relief ship was expected until sometime the following the spring.

What were they going to do? Without food and water, how were the settlers going to survive the winter?

Some turned to the Indians for help, but instead of lending a hand this time, the Indians retreated deeper into the woods away from the struggling palefaces. After all, how often had they intervened in the past to help them—only to be repaid by arrogant bullying and ridicule? No, this time, let the ungrateful newcomers fend for themselves.

By the end of December, the situation for the colonists had gone from grim to disastrous. The daily ration was soon reduced to half a pint of corn daily. According to one account, each can of corn "contained as many worms as grains."

Starving men desperately bartered their clothes and blankets for a cupful of their neighbor's corn. This resulted in many of them freezing to death as temperatures continued to drop and icy winds blasted in from the snow-packed river. Fights occasionally broke out over the dwindling supplies of food, leading to stern new laws. Anyone caught trying to steal provisions faced either having his ears cut off—or execution.

When the last few grains of corn finally disappeared, starving men and women "gladd to make shift with vermin" started eating boots, shoes, and anything else made of leather.

They crawled barefoot into the snowy woods to dig up roots and hibernating snakes for food. Some men resorted to vampirism by licking "upp the bloode which had fallen from their weak fellowes."

Besides succumbing to starvation, scores of men, women, and children were freezing to death. Houses were torn down for firewood, and even some of the wooden sections from the palisades were ripped away to chew on before throwing them onto roaring bonfires. As one writer observed: "The gates (to the settlement), no longer barred, swung back and forth in the cold winter nights..."

The most gruesome acts of survival were yet to come. As the snows of December blew into January, starving, desperate men dug up corpses from their graves and "ravenously ate them ... stewed with roots and herbs." One man actually killed his wife, salted her down, and ate part of her before his grisly crime was discovered. He was later executed.

In keeping with his bizarre Elizabethan sense of humor, Captain John Smith, the man in charge of the unfortunate colony, calmly wrote: "Whether she was better roasted, boyled or carbonado'd, I know not. But such a dish as powdered (salted) wife I never heard of."

Finally, in early March, two relief ships appeared. When Sir Thomas Gates, commander of the relief expedition, pulled into Jamestown Harbor, he was appalled at the dreary spectacle of humanity that greeted him. More dead than alive, survivors crawled and stumbled down the embankments. Instead of the five hundred settlers he had expected to find, Gates counted sixty-five "anatomies" staring back at him with terror-stricken eyes and "making pathetic sounds with their feeble voices."

"We are starved! We are starved!" they moaned, as Gates unloaded crates of food, blankets, and fresh, warm clothing. While the survivors feasted, Gates made plans to abandon the disease-haunted settlement. Some colonists favored putting the entire wretched town to the torch—an idea that Gates rejected.

The commander then ordered the handful of survivors to

climb aboard. They were going home, back to England. After three years of brutal and courageous effort, the Jamestown colonists were going to give up. Raleigh's first colony had ended in disaster; so, too, had Jamestown.

Before the ships could set sail, however, a "strange breeze" held them fast—as if some outside power were holding them back, preventing their escape. Finally, the sails caught wind and the two tiny ships with their frail and half-starved cargo of passengers lurched downriver toward the open sea.

As fate would have it, the governor of Virginia, Lord De La Warr, intercepted the ships moments before they cleared the sound. Instead of allowing them to leave, De La Warr ordered them to return to Jamestown. No one was abandoning the colony as long as he was in command! It appeared that the New World was not destined to die after all.

Diseases, famine, bad luck, broken promises, and increasingly aggressive Indian attacks would continue to plague the tiny settlement in the coming years. Of the fourteen thousand colonists who had set out to make Jamestown their home by the year 1622, thirteen thousand had died.

No war or plague in history had ever taken a higher percentage of lives than were lost during the infamous "starving time" in the fated Virginia colony.

Terror on the Natchez Trace

His name was Joseph Thompson Hare, his age unknown. No one knows where he came from, nor does anyone really know why he was hanged one dreary morning in the autumn of 1818.

Today, Hare's mortal remains rest in a lonely graveyard in Maryland, more than a thousand miles from Natchez, Mississippi, where for more than a decade his name was one of the most despised and feared along the raw frontier.

In those days—long before brightly colored steamboats chugged up and down the winding Mississippi on their way to New Orleans and the Gulf of Mexico—Hare was known as one of the most notorious outlaw-bandits operating along the infamous Natchez Trace. Before his wave of terror came to an end, this bloodthirsty villain who claimed to be a mystic with visionary powers blazed a trail of carnage up and down the historic path linking colonial Nashville with Natchez.

By his own admission, hundreds of innocent travelers had met their fate at the end of Hare's long, gleaming sword, their bones left to the buzzards and alligators along the silent, shadow-haunted Trace. The truth is, nobody will ever know just how many people Hare robbed and murdered and mutilated before his unlikely capture about 1810.

Hare, who wore fine clothes and considered himself a gentleman, attributed his remarkable success as a bandit to the spirit world. Handsome and strong, he believed "mystical forces" had guided him throughout his career as a highwayman—forces that convinced him he was a modern-day horseman of the Apocalypse.

While some contemporaries saw him as weird and fantastically religious, others believed he was Satan, sent to punish a wicked world. The cold, cruel manner in which Hare dealt with most of his hapless victims convinced law enforcement officials throughout the moss-choked bayous he was nothing more than a savage rogue, a blood-lusting butcher without a soul.

Hare's devilish reputation became his trademark. One of his favorite tactics was to hide in the bushes along the trail, then spring out whenever an unarmed stranger approached, shouting that he was the devil himself ready to drag the victim down to hell unless he turned over all his money and valuables at once. The highwayman's shameless bravura apparently worked well. Terrified travelers rarely hesitated to fork over their goods; those who held back were quickly dispatched by flashing sword or crackling gunfire. Legend has it that most of his victims—even those who cooperated—met similar fates.

On one occasion alone he reportedly took about $10,000 in gold and currency from a group of pilgrims, terrified that "the devil" was going to snatch their souls any second.

Hare's greedy exploits were, understandably, the talk of the Trace. In many ways he became the model romantic highwayman—handsome, dashing and certainly daring—as he galloped down the trail on horseback, cape flowing and sword flashing. He was well-read, and those who knew him swore there was a side to the man "so soft and sentimental, as to be almost woman-like."

From Nashville to Natchez, and on southward to New Orleans, the conversation at roadside inns, taverns, brothels, and churches centered on this marauding mystic, whom many feared more than the wild Indians, bears, alligators, and ghosts said to haunt lonely regions along the Trace. In some frontier quarters he was regarded as a folk hero, a modern-day Robin Hood who often robbed from the rich to give to the poor. Others saw him as the dangerous fiend that he was—a savage killer who would just as soon run his sword through a woman's heart as a man's.

For generations now, Hare's capture and subsequent sentence has been regarded as one of the Deep South's most troublesome mysteries. How was it, for example, that this murderous rogue, who fancied himself a psychic, mystic, ladies' man, and dandy, got off with only a five-year prison sentence? While chicken thieves and pickpockets were sent to the gallows elsewhere, Hare always managed to stay clear of the hangman's noose. Did he, as some of the old stories suggest, use spiritual forces to influence law enforcement officials? Or was it plain luck?

Even more astonishing was the manner in which he was finally apprehended.

Late one afternoon, while dozing in a cave, Hare was awakened by the tell-tale clatter of a traveler coming up the Trace. Grabbing his gun and sword, the outlaw sprang into the clearing and encountered a lone rider, a cattle drover, apparently heading back up to Nashville. With his pistol cocked and ready, Hare demanded the man's money—all of it—which the stranger happily handed over, begging that his life be spared.

For once in his life, Hare took pity on a victim. Perhaps it had something to do with the drover's own shady background. When Hare heard that the fellow was a profiteer himself, the bandit roared with uncustomary laughter and allowed his comrade-in-crime to go on his way unharmed.

As it turned out, that was Hare's biggest mistake.

Later, while making his getaway, Hare came across a strange white horse standing in the middle of the Trace. Hare described it as a "beautiful white horse, as white as snow: his ears stood straight forward and his figure was very striking."

But when the bandit approached the curious animal that seemed to shimmer in the misty gloom, it vanished right before his eyes. "When I got within six feet of him, he disappeared in an instant, which made me very uneasy." To his dying day, Hare swore that what he had seen was a spirit, a warning that he should mend his ways and repent unless he wanted to spend eternity roasting in the Lake of Fire.

Terrified by the apparition, Hare ran straight toward the nearest house, begging to be taken in for the night. The last thing he wanted to do was spend another night alone in that "whispering wilderness, full of strange spirits."

Meanwhile, the cattle drover was hot on Hare's trail. Anxious to get his money back, he had hired a couple of ruffians to help him track down the highwayman. Soon they came to the same farmhouse where Hare had taken refuge. After sneaking into his bedroom, several men grabbed him, handcuffed his hands behind him, then hauled him off to jail.

Incredibly, the "terror of the Trace"—the man responsible for the death of hundreds of innocent human beings—was tried, convicted and sent to a minimum security facility for only five years!

It was not until after Hare's release that Fate finally caught up with the once-feared beast of the Natchez Trace. For reasons that remain unclear, Hare went away to the East Coast, and wound up on the gallows in Maryland. Nobody is sure of the crime he committed there, but there is some evidence to suggest he had held up a small mail coach.

Whatever the cause, Joseph Thompson Hare received the death penalty. And on a cold, rainy afternoon, the man they called the "terror of the Trace" was blindfolded and led up a steep scaffolding toward his own date with the devil.

Christians, Cannibals, and Columbus

In the early part of the sixteenth century, Spanish explorers returning from their conquests in the New World told of horrifying encounters with strange, man-like beasts lurking in the pagan wilds of North America and among the remote, sun-splashed islands of the Caribbean.

Some of these monsters were said to have faces like dogs, and to have barked and growled at the Spanish intruders from behind bushes. Others had a single eye in the center of their foreheads and liked to slurp up the blood of comrades who had fallen in battle.

One of the most popular tales circulating in the capitals of Europe at the time concerned a mysterious race of "fish-men." These creatures supposedly had arms and legs, and looked like normal men in every way except one—they had long scaly tails and had to "dig little holes in the ground whenever they sat down."

Sometimes these "fish men" were linked to another bizarre tale—that of the "hunting fish." According to some observers, Indians in southern waters were in the habit of leashing these fish to the sides of their canoes, then releasing them to capture other fish!

The story that raised the most eyebrows dealt with an unfortunate tribe of primitives known to history as the Caribs. According to Christopher Columbus and other early voyagers, the Caribs were cannibals. Even worse, they were a particularly aggressive race of man-eaters who warred against their neighbors solely for the purpose of acquiring captives for ritualistic feeding.

Like the Aztecs of Mexico, the Caribs were fond of ripping out human organs for consumption while the victims were still conscious, perhaps drugged. Cannibalizing human flesh not only sustained these Indians during lean times, the practice also apparently enabled them to inherit the spiritual energy and strength of their enemies.

No one was safe from these man-eating marauders who roamed the Caribbean in search of fresh conquests and fresh meals. There is a possibility that some Caribs reached Florida and the Louisiana coast in their long, fast-moving canoes. Legends of cannibalistic activity among the Southeastern Indians persisted through Colonial times, though little evidence has been documented to suggest that anthropophagy—ritualistic cannibalism—was ever widespread among these native Americans.

So fierce were the Caribs, gangs of them would reportedly go into battle naked and unarmed, screaming at the top of their lungs as terror-stricken adversaries fled into the jungle. Those unable to run fast enough or who happened to be incapacitated would be rounded up, put in a pen, then later boiled or eaten alive.

When Columbus heard about these ferocious savages on his first voyage in 1492, he called them "Canibs"—a mispronunciation that would eventually result in a new word, "cannibalism" in English. The Carib Indians, therefore, had the distinction of having their name serve as a modern synonym for man-eater.

Of course, there were those who doubted the strange tales—especially when they considered the source. Most of the information about Caribs and cannibalism had been provided by a rival tribe of Indians known as the Arawaks, a docile group of natives who had befriended Columbus on his initial voyage. The Arawaks lived on the northern islands— what is modern Cuba, Puerto Rico, and Santo Domingo— while their age-old enemy, the Caribs, occupied regions farther to the south.

The Arawaks' spinning such outlandish tales about the Caribs may have had something to do with their own desperate desire to be rid of the uninvited Spaniards. Not only did they tell the bearded invaders about the Caribs, they also gave glowing accounts of fabulous cities of gold on distant islands, and of exotic creatures that talked and lived in palaces—creatures that knew the answers to many mysteries.

When the Spaniards heard such stories, their first inclination was to go see for themselves. With visions of wealth and fame burning in their helmeted heads, these gold-hungry conquistadors beat a bloody path from one island of the shimmering Caribbean to the next.

Another story about the Caribs that fascinated Europeans centered around their annual mating ritual with a mysterious tribe of female warriors known as Amazons. Each year, so the story went, selected groups of male Carib warriors would hop in their canoes and sail to the land of the Amazons for the purpose of "intercourse with the women of Martino…in which there is not a man."

Although Columbus never actually saw any evidence of cannibalism himself, he was the man responsible for spreading the rumor that man-eaters flourished in the new World. These tales, compounded by exotic and gruesome accounts of other blood-sucking humanoids and depraved female warriors, seemed to be exactly what the Catholic Church needed to later justify its Holy Inquisition in the Americas. Men or demons, fallen angels or beasts, whatever these strange creatures in the New World were, the church took upon itself the task of introducing them to the Cross—with or without their consent.

But Fate tricked the church.

Before missionaries were able to convert all the dark-skinned heathens, most of them would be dead, wiped out by diseases brought over by the Europeans. Those who survived the epidemics died later as slaves on Spanish-run sugar plantations and in silver mines.

Massacre Among the Magnolias

Tom Woolfolk was the kind of man everybody loved to hate. Not only did he have a reputation for being spoiled, lazy, and arrogant, some said he actually enjoyed being cruel to people—especially to his father's hired help.

The thing that bothered most people, though, was the way he treated his own parents. Captain and Mrs. Richard F. Woolfolk were two of the most respected and well-liked citizens in Macon, Georgia, during the late 1800s. In many ways the Woolfolks seemed the ideal family—rich, handsome, educated, and generous. They went to church, contributed regularly to charities, and gave frequent balls at their antebellum plantation on the outskirts of town.

It seemed everyone in the family was destined for greatness—except Tom.

Even as a boy Tom Woolfolk had been peculiar. Moody, restless, always whining and complaining when he didn't get his way, he was constantly getting into trouble at school and on the farm. His habits didn't improve with age, either. Unable to hold a job, Tom drifted from one hot scheme to the next, always drawing upon his father to bail him out when he ran into trouble, which was often.

On one occasion he went out west to become a cowboy. When that failed, he came back to Georgia and drove a streetcar. Several times he tried his hand at running various businesses. Nothing worked. Everything he touched seemed to fail—including marriage.

In the summer of 1887, Tom happened to meet a beautiful young socialite named Georgia Byrd, daughter of a well-to-do farmer from nearby Jones County. Legend has it that Tom proposed to Georgia on a train after secretly conspiring with a minister to be on board at the same time. The marriage lasted only three weeks. When she discovered her husband was penniless, out of work, and sponging off his father's estate, the new bride packed up her bags and drove away.

The day she left, Tom reportedly told her: "Georgia, father has not fixed me up, and I'm going to burn the family; Father's rich and got plenty; if I can't get any of it none of the others will get it."

At the time nobody made much of Tom's sullen outburst—not even his soon-to-be ex-wife.

Depressed, Tom went to work on his father's plantation for about nine dollars a week. It wasn't much, and he hated every minute of it, but at least the job kept the creditors off his back while he formulated a plan.

Sometime during the dark hours of August 6, 1887, someone broke into the isolated home of Captain and Mrs. Woolfolk and murdered the entire family. Using an axe, the killer had gone from room to room in the rambling country mansion, hacking and bludgeoning to death each member of his family—nine persons in all, including the captain and his wife, six of their children, and an elderly aunt who happened to be visiting.

The only survivor was Tom, who said he was able to escape the axe-wielding murderer by leaping out a window and running for his life.

News of the killing spread fast. Thousands of people from all over the county gathered at the plantation to witness for themselves the despicable deed. Blood and mutilated bodies lay everywhere—in the hallway, in the bathrooms, in the bedrooms where the Woolfolks had been sleeping when the killer burst in upon them. Angry citizens demanded swift justice.

The sheriff found himself in a desperate situation. One of the county's most beloved families had been wiped out by a crazed killer; he had to find a suspect and find him fast.

He didn't have far to look. Friends of the family soon convinced him that Tom Woolfolk himself was the guilty person. Newspapers were quick to pick up the accusations and glaring headlines from Atlanta to Valdosta soon began to try Tom on the front pages. "The greatest monster of the age," one newspaper called him. "The cruelest and most bloodthirsty brute on record," another proclaimed.

When angry mobs gathered at the plantation and threatened to lynch Tom, the sheriff wisely hauled the boy off to jail for his own protection. Once in custody, Tom steadfastly insisted he was innocent of the charges. "Before God and man, I am an innocent man," he reportedly told visitors to his cell.

Several bits of evidence seemed to link Tom directly with the crime. First, blood-stained clothing belonging to him had been found stuffed at the bottom of a dry well. Second, the axe used in the massacre belonged to Tom. In fact, witnesses had seen him chopping up saplings with it the day before the murder. The most damaging testimony, however, came from friends and relatives of the family who swore they had often heard Tom threaten to kill his family.

Throughout the long trial Tom continued to proclaim his innocence. While hostile crowds yelled "Hang him! Hang him!" the suspect displayed remarkable composure. "Not a muscle quivered in agitation," one observer remarked.

As the trial dragged on year after year, some people began to think perhaps Tom was innocent after all. Although the evidence itself seemed overwhelming, much of it was circumstantial in nature—not enough to convict someone legally of murder. Many Bibb Countians began to sense that perhaps they were indeed trying the wrong man. Other suspects were later brought in for questioning, but when the final verdict came in, it was as had been predicted all along— guilty on all counts.

Three years later, after several more appeals and delays, the Georgia Supreme Court sentenced Tom to hang. The date was scheduled for October 29, 1890. This was actually the third death sentence he'd received since the trial had begun. Appeals had kept him one step away from the gallows on each of the previous two occasions, but now even Tom Woolfolk knew his luck had finally run out.

At exactly one-thirty on the afternoon of October 29, the trap door was sprung and Tom Woolfolk, unshackled and unhooded, plunged to an excruciating death. Because the noose had not been knotted properly, his neck didn't break and his body continued to twitch at the end of the jerking rope for a full eleven minutes.

But at last the "bloodthirsty brute," the unloved, unsuccessful son of Captain Woolfolk, was dead, swinging from the end of a rope. The good captain and his family could now rest quietly in their graves.

Or could they?

For years after the hanging, nagging questions persisted about the guilt or innocence of Tom Woolfolk. Some people had come to the conclusion that he was incapable of having committed such a heinous crime. Others believed he had been tried and convicted unfairly in the press, and that the coverage had greatly influenced not only the jury but the presiding judge as well. And besides, hadn't he gone to the gallows maintaining his innocence? Most condemned men, fearing for their souls, make last minute confessions.

There was some evidence linking a local black man named Jack to the murder. Other suspects were now being investigated by both the authorities and the newspapers. Some publishers had begun to wonder if perhaps they had attacked the wrong man in their unrelenting editorial crusade for justice.

The mystery doesn't end there.

Years after the hanging, a legend grew that Tom Woolfolk had not been executed, but that the sheriff and some other friends of the family had secretly conspired to help him escape. There were several accounts in local newspapers about a man fitting Woolfolk's description living in Texas at the turn of the century.

Like those of John Wilkes Booth, Jesse James, and others, the legend of Tom Woolfolk became ingrained in the folklore of the South.

Voodoo Queens
and Sleeping Prophets

Edgar Cayce:
"America's Most Mysterious Man"

On the night of April 18, 1900, a young Kentucky photographer named Edgar Cayce suddenly lost his voice. His condition was diagnosed as "paralysis of the vocal organs," and it was doubtful he would ever speak again.

Unwilling to accept such a fate, Cayce turned desperately to hypnosis for relief. At the time, hypnosis was still a relatively new branch of science and very few doctors were trained in its application. Of those trained, fewer still were willing to use it.

But Cayce finally found a physician who agreed to take the chance. After ten months of hypnotic therapy, the 23-year-old photographer's voice finally returned. It seemed a miracle at the time, but the truly amazing thing is what happened to him during those long hours of treatment each day.

Whenever he went into a trance, this shy, sensitive, deeply religious man who dropped out of school in the seventh grade would talk about things far beyond his range of knowledge and expertise. In fact, he would often discuss complex medical matters, drawing upon principles, theories, and terminologies unknown outside the medical and scientific community.

In no time, Cayce was astounding the academic world with his pinpoint diagnoses and recommended remedies for other patients, some of whom were hospitalized hundreds of miles away. Cayce was even credited for having identified and prescribed the treatment that eventually led to his own cure.

It didn't take long for news of this amazing "healer" to spread across the country. Newspapers and magazines were quick to pick up on the Cayce story, and soon banner headlines were proclaiming him "America's Most Mysterious Man." One paper wrote: "Edgar Cayce Startles Medical Men With His Trances."

As for himself, Cayce was startled by all the hoopla. Even more confounding, he couldn't remember any of the things he was credited with having said while under hypnosis! It was as if somebody else would step inside his body and speak for him, some highly trained doctor of medicine whose authoritative voice rumbled with confidence and wisdom.

Gradually Cayce came to appreciate his unusual mediumistic powers. Shortly after his remarkable recovery, he discovered that by lying down, thoroughly relaxing, and taking a deep breath, he could duplicate the trances on his own. In such self-induced states, Cayce's voice would boom across the room, diagnosing problems and prescribing remedies for patients and visitors who flocked to him from all over the South.

There now had merged two Cayces—a "waking" Cayce, the reclusive, soft-spoken photographer, and the "sleeping" Cayce, the psychic healer the media were now calling the "sleeping prophet."

Over the next several decades Edgar Cayce would delight and astonish the world with his accurate and often reassuring predictions about future events. But most people came to his office for "healing" purposes—about 16,000 between 1901 and 1944. Copies of most of his readings are still on file in the archives of the Association for Research and Enlightenment, an institute set up at Virginia Beach, Virginia, to study Cayce's unique powers.

In all that time, there was never an indication that Cayce was conscious of a single word he uttered while in the self-imposed hypnotic state. Even though Cayce couldn't account for this himself, he theorized that the thousands of readings and predictions apparently came through or out of his unconscious mind.

By 1913, Cayce's fame as the "sleeping prophet" had reached international proportions. Hundreds of people visited his office each year, some from as far away as Europe and Asia. Each day his office was flooded with requests for special readings that usually involved healing, although a few preferred "psychic readings." The telephone rang constantly, as did the doorbell.

Cayce, a self-taught preacher of the strictest integrity and character, rarely charged for his psychic services. But his conditions were strict: an appointment would have to be set up for 11 a.m. or 3 p.m. on a specified day. The applicant did not have to be present, but it was necessary that Cayce be given the person's real name and address—and where that individual would be at the specified time of reading.

Cayce's own routine never varied. He would come in from the garden or from fishing, loosen his tie, shoelaces, cuffs, and belt, then lie down on a couch. His hands would be placed first palm-up on his forehead, then across his abdomen. Drawing in deep gulps of air several times, he would close his eyes and relax. When his eyelids began to flutter, the reading would begin.

Afterwards, he might sleep for a couple hours or more. He would awaken—refreshed—without remembering a single thing about the reading.

In the early 1920s, the "sleeping prophet" became obsessed with reincarnation. Often, when tracking patients' previous lives, Cayce would take them hundreds or thousands of years into the past. Occasionally he would link them to the lost continent of Atlantis, where he proclaimed some of their "spiritual entities" had been born.

Some of Cayce's readings about Atlantis received special attention from the press. Not since Plato had anyone spoken with so much authority about the fabled landmass that supposedly sank beneath the waves during a cataclysmic upheaval some twelve thousand years ago. According to Cayce, who "visited" Atlantis hundreds of times during his trances, runaway technology was the cause for its demise.

In 1936 he wrote:

"In Atlantean land just after the second breaking up of the land owing to misapplication of divine laws upon those things of nature or of the earth; when there were the eruptions from the second using of those influences that were for man's own development, yet becoming destructive forces to flesh when misapplied."

Before their land was destroyed, Atlanteans had developed a kind of nuclear energy superior to modern-day technology. "Rays...invisible to the eye" propelled vehicles through the air and beneath the sea, Cayce said.

Upon waking, Cayce was sometimes startled, even embarrassed, at some of his readings. A religious man who read the Bible every day, the last thing he wanted was for anybody to accuse him of being un-Christian. He was especially troubled about his comments on reincarnation, though day after day, reading after reading, his sleeping self always kept coming back to the subject.

Although Cayce's "life readings" on reincarnation and Atlantis deviated from his normal "healing" sessions, he would remain fascinated with those subjects for the rest of his life. In fact, Cayce's peculiar work in the field has been quoted numerous times by scientists, theologians, spiritualists and other investigators in the field of paranormal research.

Even more startling, one of Cayce's most famous revelations about Atlantis would come true, just as he had predicted in the 1940s. During one of his trances, he said that in the late 1960s the western region of the long-submerged continent of Atlantis would begin to appear near the Caribbean island of Bimini.

In 1968, just a few miles from Bimini, divers came across a group of undersea ruins that resembled collapsed buildings and some kind of ancient roadway system. Could this be the remains of the vanished Atlantean civilization?

Many followers of Edgar Cayce believe his most startling prophecy had come to pass.

In 1945, Cayce went to his grave still unaware of his unique contributions to the field of paranormal science.

In Search of Ambrose Bierce

Early one morning in the autumn of 1913, a 71-year-old grandfather rose from his bed, saddled the family horse, and then quietly and secretively rode away from his home near Washington, D.C.

He headed south, first stopping off at famous Civil War battlefields in Tennessee and Mississippi before passing through Louisiana and Texas on his way to the badlands of war-torn Mexico. His goal, as far as anyone has been able to determine, was to join up with a gang of revolutionaries led by Generalissimo Francisco "Pancho" Villa.

But somewhere along the way this aged, would-be soldier of fortune vanished. He was never seen or heard from again, and today, almost eight decades later, people the world over are still intrigued by the mysterious circumstances surrounding the disappearance of Ambrose Bierce, one of America's foremost journalists and tellers of tall tales.

Bierce's fate remains one of the literary world's most enduring and fascinating mysteries. So many theories have cropped up over the years to account for his demise they would probably fill a small library.

For years newspaper reporters, detectives, and secret service agents from the United States combed the rugged hinterlands of Mexico and Latin America for clues to the missing writer's fate. Not a trace of the elderly man was ever found again, leading one biographer to conclude that Bierce had "simply but stylishly vanished from the face of the earth."

Whatever happened, it is highly unlikely that Bierce—

whose gloomy, nihilistic works include *The Devil's Diction-ary; In the Midst of Life; Fantastic Fables;* and *Can Such Things Be?*—would have been flattered by all the hoopla surrounding his curious destiny. Interest in the Bierce legend soon reached international levels, eclipsing that of his books and columns.

As Clifton Fadiman, the noted essayist, once remarked, "Bierce was never a great writer anyway. He has painful faults of vulgarity and cheapness of imagination. But...his style, for one thing, will preserve him...and the purity of his misan-thropy, too, will help to keep him alive."

Gloomy, morose, melancholy, sarcastic, bitter—these words have all been used to describe the man whom critics and colleagues alike once dubbed "Bitter Bierce" because of his fierce, uncompromising literary assaults on what he con-sidered a depraved and morally bankrupt society. He attacked hypocrisy, especially, wherever he found it—from the halls of Congress to the sanctuaries of churches and cathedrals everywhere.

He railed against big business and the military, preferring to champion the causes of the poor and downtrodden. In his day, Bierce was regarded as a minor prophet of hopelessness, a fiery, pessimistic fellow whose impassioned pen unleashed a flood of temperamental tirades against government, big business, religion, and "that old devil" progress.

Born in a log cabin in Ohio, Bierce fought bravely on the side of the North during the Civil War, but always sympa-thized with the aristocratic planter-culture in the antebellum South. After the war—which would greatly influence his later writing—Bierce settled in San Francisco where he found a job with the *News Letter,* of which he eventually became editor.

In 1871 he married and went to London to work as a correspondent. It was there that the stinging nature of his work emerged, along with the nickname "Bitter Bierce."

Because of a life-long asthma problem, he moved back to San Francisco in 1876, and from 1887 to 1896 wrote a column for the *San Francisco Examiner* before accepting a position with *Cosmopolitan* in Washington, D.C.

Ambrose Bierce was never a happy man. Dead ends, failures, and tragedies haunted his personal life. In 1889 his son was killed in a vulgar shooting brawl over a girl; two years later his wife left him, finally divorcing him in 1904; in 1901 his youngest son died of alcoholism; and in 1913 Bierce—old, asthmatic, weary, his creative power only an acrid memory—made his queer escape from civilization, presumably to Mexico where he met his fate.

Though never great, Bierce's writings were read, and after the events of his strange disappearance were made known, they soared in popularity. The stories, assembled in book-length collections, ranged from the supernatural and horror to the grotesquely humorous.

His acidic dislike for and lack of patience with the human race stains the pages of most of his writing, including his most famous short piece, "An Occurrence At Owl Creek Bridge," which was made into a television film. Seeking to capitalize on a resurging interest in the Bierce phenomenon, Hollywood recently released a $24 million movie of Carlos Fuentes' novel *The Old Gringo,* starring Gregory Peck as the reclusive, controversial writer.

"Nobody will find my bones," Bierce once wrote. Little did he know how prophetic those words would be when, at the ripe old age of 71, he took off for Mexico, ostensibly to observe the revolution then rocking that nation. "I'm on my way to Mexico," he told a reporter. "I like the fighting...I want to see it."

As years passed, people on both sides of the Rio Grande speculated on his death. Did he commit suicide, as some experts claim? Did he succumb to natural causes, such as the asthma that had plagued him all his life? Was he shot by Pancho Villa or some other renegade Mexican officer?

Some say he never died in Mexico at all—that he made his way to England or perhaps back to his old home in California. One writer even theorized that he spent his last years in an asylum for the insane in California.

Whatever the truth, Ambrose Bierce's curious fate remains as mystifying as was his own unfathomable life.

The Mystery of Marie Laveau's Tomb

For more than a century now, visitors to New Orleans have been flocking to a lonely, moss-draped cemetery just north of the French Quarter to ponder over one of that city's most enduring mysteries.

Within the graveyard, buried beneath a crumbling brick tomb, are the remains of an old woman who died sometime around 1881. There are no dates on the inscription—only the French phrase: *"Famille Vve. Paris, neé Laveau."*

According to legend, the grave in question contains the mortal remains of Marie Laveau, the beautiful but notorious voodoo queen who brought fear and death to New Orleans throughout much of the 19th century.

Until a few years ago, no one doubted the legend. After all, there had been a funeral in St. Louis Cemetery No. 1, and hundreds of people from all across the country had come to pay final respects to one of New Orleans' most colorful and mysterious characters.

Now, however, there is some evidence to suggest that the infamous queen might not have been buried in her assigned grave after all. Instead, it appears likely that the vivacious hobgoblin's mortal remains were interred in an unmarked grave elsewhere—perhaps not even in the same cemetery.

According to some historians who have looked into the matter, Laveau's body was dug up shortly after the funeral and moved to a secret location to avoid having the grave turned into a kind of shrine for her legions of white-robed followers.

If this is so, then two questions naturally arise—who is really buried inside Laveau's tomb? And, more importantly, where is the high priestess of New Orleans voodoo actually buried?

To understand the mystery of Laveau's tomb, it might be helpful to review some of the facts and fallacies about the queen's storied life and times.

In her heyday, Laveau was the undisputed ruler of the voodoo cult, a mystical, quasi-religious organization that attracted thousands of followers, black and white. While she reigned supreme in New Orleans no one was safe from her unrelenting supernatural powers—not even aristocratic white planters who often came to her in the dead of night for secret sessions involving voodoo and, some say, sex.

It was also said that Laveau, a tall, striking woman with fiercely burning eyes, controlled her subjects in two main ways—by blowing "magic dust" in their faces and by exploiting their fear of the unseen world. In the minds of most blacks, freshly transplanted from the jungles of Africa via the Caribbean, ghosts and goblins stalked the streets of the city and haunted the surrounding woods and marshes.

For these blacks, most of them slaves or poor freedmen, it was a world of darkness and unrelenting terror, a world filled with unimaginable nightmares. The angry gods of voodoo were everywhere.

To protect themselves from voodoo and to ward off other evil spirits, the faithful flocks were compelled to purchase powders, herbs and talismans—usually from a *hougon,* or voodoo priest, or from the high priestess herself, Marie Laveau. Although the authorities tried to suppress voodoo in most parts of the city, they largely ignored the strange dancing, chanting, and bonfires burning in black quarters.

By all accounts, the voodoo cult had been firmly implanted in New Orleans by the early colonial period, but it was not until the arrival of Marie Laveau that the practice of this enigmatic religion blossomed. Up until then it was known that certain voodoo priests and priestesses possessed supernatural powers and a knowledge of mind-altering drugs and poisons. White masters were sometimes powerless when under the influence of voodoo spells, and there are some records of slave owners having been poisoned by drug-influenced blacks.

It was into such a fear-haunted world that Laveau was born one cold, rainy night in 1796. Legend has it that on that night a terrible storm blew in from the swamps, shaking the moss-draped trees and howling across quaint cobblestoned squares.

Marie was a free mulatto, a status which gave her certain privileges around town. When she was in her early twenties, she married another mulatto named Jacques Paris. After Paris's death, Laveau had a daughter, whom she also named Marie. In time, the daughter would succeed her mother as the exalted voodoo queen, thereby creating a mystery that only recently has been solved.

Because of the secret succession in leadership of the cult, it was erroneously assumed that the original Marie Laveau was immortal, that she somehow had been able to cheat death and old age. The mother-daughter reign confused not only her superstitious followers but future generations of historians as well.

It was the older Laveau, however, who is credited with having established her place at the head of the cult. Not long after she had joined as a low-ranking member following her husband's death, Laveau quickly usurped Sanite Dede's place as queen. Beautiful, strong and supremely resourceful, Laveau set about to transform the cult into a powerful but curious mixture of West Indian fetish-worship and perverted Catholicism.

A devout Roman Catholic herself, Laveau continued to attend mass daily while retaining her exalted office as queen of voodoo.

Throughout her life, Laveau welcomed outsiders to her cult's annual festival on St. John's Eve in midsummer, but behind these public ceremonies, Marie Laveau presided over many secret meetings during which the real magic of voodoo was invoked and the wild ritual carried to orgiastic extremes.

Whites were excluded from these meetings, which were usually held at her small, white-washed house along the gloomy shores of Lake Pontchartrain.

The first Marie Laveau stopped practicing sometime around 1869, at which time her daughter assumed the duties of queenship. A power struggle would later develop between the younger Laveau and a powerful young rival, Malvina Latour. According to some experts, Latour eventually won the fight. If this is true, then it seems entirely possible that the grave at St. Louis Cemetery No. 1 contains her bones—not those of Marie Laveau.

Others say, however, that the remains are those of the younger Laveau.

No one knows for sure.

The Twilight World of Robert Ervin Howard

In the summer of 1936 Robert Ervin Howard had everything to live for. He was young, handsome, and on the verge of literary fame. After years of rejection notices and only a handful of published short stories, things were definitely starting to look up for the young writer.

Then, inexplicably, the tranquility of tiny Cross Plains, Texas, a wind-blown community in the middle of nowhere, was shattered by the sound of a gunshot. Eight hours later, one of the town's most famous sons—and one of America's greatest writers of fantasy fiction—was dead, the victim of an apparent suicide.

Howard was only thirty.

As the swaggering, hard-drinking creator of Conan the Barbarian and dozens of other "sword-and-sorcery" epics, Robert E. Howard was just beginning to make a name for himself in the literary world. Magazine editors were now calling him for stories, and several of his book-length projects were being considered by a major publisher.

Why, then, did this brooding, wildly eccentric man bristling with ambition and talent suddenly decide to end it all with a bullet?

Howard's untimely death and the mystery behind it have haunted his legions of fans for more than fifty years. Based on the writer's own typewritten suicide note and several other factors, no one disputes the notion that the man did in all probability kill himself, and that no one else was involved.

What troubles a lot of people, however, are the circumstances leading up to his suicide. Friends, fellow writers, and fans over the years have long pondered those circumstances, and to this day, have failed to reach a consensus.

Was it fear of failure that finally drove him to put the Colt .380 automatic pistol to his right temple that hot, humid day in June, or was it just the opposite—fear of success? Some researchers have suggested the man was driven insane by the same tortured fantasies that gave life to his most celebrated fictional hero, Conan.

The most likely cause, however, was that he dreaded the thought of being left alone in a world he never really understood. His mother, with whom he shared an unnaturally close relationship, was dying. Three times before, he had planned his own demise when her death appeared imminent, but each time the old woman had rallied.

Finally, when a nurse told the grieving son his mother would never recognize him again, he acted. His final enigmatic words, left on the typewriter in his study, were these:

All fled—all is done, so lift me on the pyre:
The feast is over and the lamps expire.

Although Howard's death fell short of national headlines, thousands of people around the world mourned his passing. Scores of fans flocked into town to attend his funeral. Over the years, thousands more would come to Cross Plains to pay tribute to their fallen idol, to remember a man now regarded as one of the masters of the genre.

All his short life, Howard had dreamed of a world far beyond the dusty confines of his little hometown. Through the magic of his writing, Howard was able to bring that visionary, fire-filled world to literary life. He called it the Hyborian Age, a savage, barbarous time when magic was potent, chesty heroes clutched swords, and big-bosomed damsels lived according to their own personal codes.

One character dominated the age—a man whose body was "an image of primal strength cut out of bronze," who liked his women full-bodied and complacent but spent most of his time "afire with the urge to kill, to drive his knife deep into flesh and bone, and twist the blade in blood entrails."

That character, of course, was Conan.

Conan the Barbarian, who stalked the earth twelve thousand years ago, was only one of Howard's many swashbuckling, sword-rattling protagonists. He was the most enduring, however, eventually finding immortality in the person of Arnold Schwarzenegger on the silver screen.

Altogether he wrote sixty stories and novels, of which about twenty-one were developed around his brutish, slow-thinking hero.

Even so, fame and fortune always stayed one step beyond the struggling young writer. It wasn't until the 1940s, nearly a decade after his death, that Conan and his barbarian hordes actually earned literary respectability. The biggest break came in 1966 when a leading paperback publisher issued the first of what was to become a hugely successful series of Conan adventure novels—not all of them written by Howard.

In many ways, Howard's short, dream-haunted life was every bit as mystifying and as frightening as anything he wrote. Born frail and sickly, he was forced to learn boxing early in order to defend himself against other kids. He also took an interest in body-building, which probably helped shape his interest in Conan.

He started writing stories when he was ten, pushing himself ruthlessly on the typewriter day and night. When his first story was purchased by *Weird Tales* in 1924, the eighteen-year-old got down on his knees and thanked God he'd finally broken into print.

Only twelve years later, despondent over his mother's death, wracked by nightmares, and undoubtedly pursued by the fiendish demons of his own fevered fantasies, Robert E. Howard lay dying in a pool of blood behind his beloved mother's house.

Can Such Things Be?

The Sargasso: Graveyard of the Sea

Just off the southern tip of the United States, and veering east by northeast for thousands of square miles, is a vast, weed-choked range of open sea that for centuries has haunted the imagination of mariners on both sides of the Atlantic.

This is the Sargasso Sea, home to some of the world's most unusual flora and fauna. It is here, thousands of miles from their normal habitat, that American and European eels make their mysterious journey each year to breed and lay eggs amid the cool, clear waters and fearsome tangles of sargassum weed.

It is also here that one of the world's most enduring mysteries has developed.

Every schoolchild knows about the Sargasso Sea, the fabled "graveyard of lost ships," where—according to maritime lore—the rotting remains of thousands of unfortunate ocean voyagers lie trapped and forever entombed aboard their stalled ships in dense, gloomy forests of monstrous vegetation.

Legend has it that this is a dead world with no storms, wind or waves to ever break them free. Victims who happen to get caught up in the twisting, treacherous coils of the sargassum weed are doomed, so the stories go, to drift helplessly upon the unyielding sea for all eternity. Like snapshots out of history, the skeletal ribs of Spanish galleons, steam freighters, Yankee clippers, frigates, Chinese junks, Roman triremes, and even Norse dragonships still struggle in the embrace of octopus-like vines, their rudders and propellers held fast by gigantic weeds and tree-thick roots.

Until recent times, the mere thought of coming upon the Sargasso Sea was enough to weaken even the strongest sailor. Even during the American Revolution, and later during the Civil War, sea captains kept a constant lookout for signs of danger when entering the Sargasso. Stories were often told about wayward ships getting caught in those entangling currents, never to be seen or heard from again.

In July 1884, for example, the *Brittania,* bound for London from Buenos Aires, came across a merchant ship that had apparently been abandoned in the Sargasso. There were a few corpses on board, but most of the crew and passengers were missing.

Nowadays it is known that the dreaded sea, which covers nearly three million square miles between North America and Europe, is actually one of the safest places in the entire ocean. Warm currents and calm winds prevail over still, glass-smooth waters, and only occasionally does an ocean-going vessel come in contact with the once-feared sargassum weed.

Such was not the case five hundred years ago when the man who discovered North America first laid eyes on the mysterious Sargasso Sea.

It happened in 1492, during Christopher Columbus's first voyage to the New World. Somewhere far out in the Atlantic, a thousand miles west of the Azores, he spotted what he took to be long strands of seaweeds, stretching as far as the eye could see in every direction. At first, the veteran Genoan sea captain took heart at the sighting, thinking that perhaps his tiny flotilla was at last nearing land.

But his optimism soon turned to terror when he realized just how thick grew the ancient weeds, how twisted and gnarled were their branches and ominous coils. To his dismay, he felt the temperature quickly sink, and the ocean seemed to stand utterly still.

This is the chilling account Columbus gave of that and subsequent experiences in the Sargasso Sea:

"Each time I sailed from Spain to the Indies...I noticed an extraordinary change in the aspect of the sky and the stars, in the temperature of the air and in that of the sea. I found the surface of the water covered so thickly with vegetation resembling small branches of fir that we believed we must be in shallow waters and that the ships would soon be aground for lack of depth...."

More than any other factor, Columbus's grim account about the perils of the Sargasso Sea helped inspire the terror that would fill the hearts of future generations of seafaring peoples. Fear of the Sargasso and its clutching embrace of death soon became an obsession with sailors and ocean-going travelers everywhere.

No one wanted his ship to become ensnared in those treacherous masses of enveloping weed, for no wind would ever come to the rescue, and no kind wave would wash it away. Tales about the Sargasso were circulated and re-circulated below deck and among the waterfront taverns and inns from the Outer Banks to Land's End.

Before long, novels and newspaper stories began to appear, each as frightening and disturbing as the next. "The Island of Lost Ships" explored the possibility that cannibalistic survivors could actually exist among the wreckage and ruin of the Sargasso, preying upon newcomers. Thomas Alliborne Janvier also wrote about similar discoveries in his book *In the Sargasso Sea;* other novels led readers to believe that the Sargasso is actually part of the lost continent of Atlantis, and that descendants of that civilization still live in the Sargasso region today.

Much attention has been focused on the fact that the geographic boundaries of the Sargasso Sea approximate the whereabouts of ancient Atlantis. As if this weren't fanciful enough, the western edge of the large, singular sea touches on the edge of the Bermuda Triangle, scene of many strange maritime events over the years. Incredibly, some of the ships and planes that have gone missing in the Triangle region have been linked to mysterious forces in the Sargasso Sea.

In spite of the many myths shrouding this swirling body of water far out in the Atlantic, scientists agree that the Sargasso itself is an ocean wonder. Some of the world's oldest flora and fauna abound here—including the sargassum weed, capable of surviving for hundreds of years in the unusual climate of the Sargasso.

The Sargasso is also the breeding ground for several species of fish, including American and European eels which swim thousands of miles each year to mate in its frothy seaweed forests. This bizarre ritual has given rise to speculation that the Sargasso region was indeed once home to an ancient landmass, perhaps Atlantis, and that these migrating eels somehow still share a genetic memory of those distant days.

Today, modern ships cross the Sargasso Sea every day without trouble. But the mystery of this haunting region lives on, and despite the testimony of some questionable sources, no evidence exists to suggest that any vessel, ancient or modern, has ever been lost in the Sargasso Sea.

Florida's Fabled Fountain of Youth

In the spring of 1513, an aging Spanish conquistador named Juan Ponce de León set sail from his Caribbean home in search of a mysterious land called Florida and its legendary fountain of youth.

Or did he?

Historians aren't so sure that the tall, dashing, 50-year-old governor of Puerto Rico had ever even heard of a fountain of youth, let alone made it the focus of his three-year exploratory voyage around the coastal wilds of Florida. Instead, it now appears that Ponce de León—the first European known to have set foot on Florida soil—was actually looking for slaves and gold when he planted the flag of Spain on a sandy shore near modern-day Cape Canaveral.

What apparently happened was that a highly imaginative historian named Herrera, who chronicled Ponce de León's exploits in the New World years after the event, had come across a fanciful Indian legend about a mysterious stream of water located somewhere north of Cuba that supposedly had the power to restore youth. In order to make his accounts more exciting—and, perhaps, to earn a bigger name for himself—Herrera attached the legend to Ponce de León's name and subsequent voyages of discovery.

According to Herrera, the governor had heard about the legend from various tribes of Caribbean Indians and decided to investigate. Part of that legend centered around a group of Arawaks who supposedly migrated from Cuba northward because of a magical river where "life-giving waters flowed pure and plenty."

Today, southeastern scholars discount that story, even though numerous other legends in the New World tell of similar such streams located somewhere in the vast wilds of North America.

But Herrera, who liked dramatic storytelling more than dull history, milked the legend for all it was worth. He insisted that Ponce de León, concerned about his waning years, went to Florida to find, then drink and bathe in the fountain.

It wasn't the first mistake made by the unreliable historian—and it wouldn't be the last. For example, he incorrectly reported that Ponce de León waded ashore on Easter Sunday in the year 1513 just south of Fort Lauderdale. Evidence now shows that the conquistador was still at sea on Easter Sunday, and that he actually landed on the Florida coast much farther south than was generally believed— perhaps near modern-day Cape Canaveral.

Researchers, all too aware of Herrera's zealous pen, say there is nothing in the pages of the conquistador's original patent from Emperor Charles V to suggest anything but a businesslike expedition to explore and perhaps colonize the Florida peninsula. Nor are there indications from subsequent records to suggest that Ponce de León had the slightest notion about the curious fountain which would follow his name down through the ages.

What is known is that the once-wealthy governor was seeking to replenish his lost fortune by finding gold and capturing Indians to sell as slaves to colonial plantation owners.

In spite of all the evidence to the contrary, Ponce de León's exalted name continues to be linked with the fabled fountain of youth. However erroneous, it is a wonderful, romantic tale that simply won't go away. Part of the allure has been perpetuated by generations of profit-hungry real estate developers and land speculators in Florida who in former years sought to capitalize on the legend.

For centuries, people were drawn to the "land of

flowers" in search of that same magical stream whose bubbling waters were said to have the power to restore youth. According to stories handed down by the Indians and undoubtedly kept alive by developers, just one sip of or dip into the stream would wash away wrinkles.

The existence of Ponce de León's wondrous stream, real or imagined, turned out to be a marketing gold mine for land developers and speculators from Tallahassee to Hialeah. Soon not even hurricanes, droughts, renegade Indians, or dense tracts of swampland teeming with mosquitoes, alligators, and poisonous snakes could hold back the hordes of prosperous northerners looking for investment in the South.

Almost overnight, Florida was transformed from a sleepy backwater draw to the vacationland of the future. From swampgrass to golf courses, primitive mud huts to glistening beachfront high-rises, the "land of flowers" would never be the same again.

Where was the fabled fountain? Some historians say the legend had its origins in northern Florida, while others say it was in Georgia or Alabama. Still others claim it was on the island of Guanahani (San Salvador) or on Bimini. Only a few experts insist it was in the Everglades, as originally believed.

In the event such a stream ever existed, one can rightfully suspect it is no longer there—drained away, perhaps, or bulldozed over to make room for a parking lot or glittering row of condominiums.

Flight 19's Date with the Unknown

On the afternoon of December 5, 1945, five TBM Avenger torpedo bombers took off from their home base at Fort Lauderdale, Florida, on a two-hour training flight that would carry them eastward to Grand Bahama Island and back, a distance of about three hundred forty miles.

Aboard the lead plane was Lt. Charles Carroll Taylor, one of only two experienced officers on the mission. The twelve other crewmen—pilots, radiomen and gunners—were all students in training.

The weather was cold but surprisingly clear for that time of year. Only a trace of fog hovered offshore as Flight 19 lifted off from Lauderdale Naval Air Station and headed toward its target, a practice bombing range called Chicken Shoals, just north of Bimini.

Less than half an hour after the successful bombing run, something unexpected happened. At precisely 3:15, the radio tower back at Fort Lauderdale, which had been expecting contact from the planes regarding estimated time of arrival, received an unusual message from the flight leader.

"Both my compasses are out," the leader, Lt. Taylor, reported urgently. "This is an emergency. We seem to be off course. We cannot land...Repeat...We cannot see land."

Puzzled, the tower advised Flight 19 to continue on course bearing due west. To which Lt. Taylor replied: "We don't know which way is west. Everything is wrong-...Strange...We can't be sure of any direction—even the ocean doesn't look as it should."

Communications later broke down with Flight 19. Not long afterwards, a Martin Mariner rescue plane with a crew of thirteen was dispatched to the general area. Inexplicably, the rescue plane, too, vanished without a trace over the blue-green Atlantic.

As for Flight 19, a five-day search covering 380,000 square miles of land and sea, including the Atlantic, Caribbean, parts of the Gulf of Mexico, and the Florida mainland and neighboring islands, failed to discover any trace of the airplanes or their crew. No life rafts, no wreckage, and no tell-tale oil slicks were found, in spite of continued air and sea searches along the beaches of Florida and the Bahamas for several more weeks.

It was as if Flight 19, along with the flying boat sent out from Miami to rescue its crew, had simply vanished into thin air.

In those days, only a few months after World War II, the warm waters off the Florida coast were a tranquil region, a favored training area for combat-weary sailors and aviators. But in time, as more and more airplanes and ships vanished mysteriously there, that perception would change. Soon a whole new folklore would develop around that peculiar patch of sea that came to be known as the Bermuda Triangle.

Since 1945, more than one hundred ships and planes—many of them in full view of witnesses—have vanished without a trace in or over the Bermuda Triangle. At least a thousand people have lost their lives in that enigmatic area since the five Navy Grumman TBM-3 Avenger torpedo bombers of Flight 19 flew off into the unknown. Ironically, not a single body or piece of wreckage from any of these lost ships and planes has ever been recovered.

Not surprisingly, an aura of profound mystery now shrouds this expanse of open sea where so many ships and planes have gone down without explanation. Many theories, some of them admittedly fanciful, have evolved to account for these disappearances, ranging from supernatural involvement to extraterrestrial connections. Most explanations have been linked to sudden tidal waves caused by earthquakes, exploding fireballs, attacks by sea monsters, time-space warps, electromagnetic or gravitational vortices, and, of course, capture or kidnapping by unidentified flying objects.

Today the Bermuda Triangle is regarded by many as one of the most dangerous maritime regions on earth. Even the U.S. Coast Guard describes it as "an imaginary area located off the southeastern Atlantic coast...which is noted for a high incidence of unexplained losses of ships, small boats, and aircraft...."

Even long before 1945, the Bermuda Triangle had been regarded in maritime circles as a secretive, eerie place (probably contributing to legends about a "lost sea" or the legendary "ship's graveyard" of yore). Some disappearances actually were reported after the Civil War, but it wasn't until the episode involving Flight 19 that the Bermuda Triangle became a household term.

To be sure, hardly a year goes by without some report of a ship or plane going astray in that troublesome triangle extending from Bermuda in the north to southern Florida, then east through the Bahamas past Puerto Rico to about 40° west longitude, and then back again to Bermuda. This is made even more bizarre, given the fact that sealanes and airways are busier now, and rescue technology is far more advanced.

The fate of Flight 19, as well as that of the hundred or so other known planes, ships, and hot-air balloons lost over the Bermuda Triangle, remains one of the South's greatest unsolved mysteries.

The Curse of Barnsley Gardens

As a young man growing up in Savannah, Godfrey Barnsley dreamed of someday owning his own cotton plantation.

That dream came true in the late 1830s when the wealthy businessman acquired what he considered an ideal spread—a 10,000-acre tract of virgin timberland and rolling fields near Adairsville in the northwest corner of Georgia.

As fate would have it, greed, the Civil War, and an old Indian curse would soon combine to turn Barnsley's dream into a nightmare.

In those days, more than two decades before the War Between the States, the woods and hills of remote Bartow County still swarmed with roaming bands of Indians, many of them outlaws and renegades from the infamous Trail of Tears. Understandably, many resented the encroachment of white settlers into their ancestral territory and resisted any way they could.

One particular old chief, who happened to live on Barnsley's new property, was so angered that legend has it he put a curse on the white man and on the very ground on which he planned to build his sprawling plantation house.

Nobody thought much about the curse, nor about rumors that the Barnsley estate was said to contain a mysterious, acorn-shaped hill feared by the Cherokees. Life went on somewhat uneventfully for the next few months, and soon Barnsley brought his wife and family to his property to live.

Then, only days before the manor house was completed, Barnsley's wife Julia and their infant son died mysteriously while living in temporary shelter on the accursed grounds.

The planter was heartbroken by his loss, but completed the house anyway and moved in with his surviving daughter and son.

The curse was forgotten—until the autumn of 1858 when Barnsley's teenage daughter also died in the house. That same year, his son was killed by Chinese pirates while the young man searched the Orient for exotic plants for the estate's formal gardens.

By then the unfortunate planter was beside himself with grief and worry. He sought out mediums, psychics, and religious leaders to help undo what the old Indian had done to him long ago, but his pleas fell on deaf ears since white people apparently did not understand Indian magic.

Barnsley's troubles did not end with the sad demise of his family members. Beginning in late 1860, one business venture after another failed. Barnsley's once sizeable fortune had soon been reduced to a pathetic fraction of its former worth. A few months later, with the outbreak of war, the miserable planter was left alone with his unfinished manor house and a ruined cotton-buying operation.

Barnsley's once-handsome estate now lay in shambles, along with his dream of becoming one of the most prosperous planters in the South.

On his deathbed, Barnsley reportedly begged a minister to rid his property of its evil curse. It was too late to bring back his family, of course, or to restore his health and fortune, but at least he hoped future owners would be spared misfortune and grief.

In the summer of 1989, almost 150 years after Barnsley set out to establish his cotton empire in the foothills of Georgia, another Cherokee returned to the estate to undo the old chief's curse. Richard Bird, a medicine man from Cherokee, North Carolina, said he knew something was wrong the moment he stepped onto the property.

"There was definitely something here when we got here—there was something," he told reporters. "I had a funny feeling inside—I can't explain it. It was kind of a nervousness, like butterflies in my stomach, like a cold sweat."

Bird was hired to perform a "casting out" ceremony by an attorney representing the estate's new owner, Stonewall Limited Partnership, which is developing the property known locally now as Woodlands.

Bird thinks his services were unnecessary. He said that any curse put on the property died along with the old Indian himself.

"When a person dies, his magic is no longer good," he explained.

Even so, at the new property owner's insistence, he performed the ancient ritual of casting off conjurations anyway—"just to be on the safe side," he said.

Ghost Lights in the Forest

One hot summer night in the early 1960s, Chester McMinn was out plowing his field near Quapaw, Oklahoma, when suddenly, at the far edge of the woods, there appeared a strange blue light flickering among the pines.

As the farmer watched from his tractor, the eerie light began to dance and weave, dreamlike in the distance. Then, still bobbing and swirling, the light headed slowly toward him, becoming brighter as it moved.

McMinn shuddered. It was almost as if the thing had *sensed* his presence and was coming over to investigate!

Within seconds the spooky blue light was directly overhead. The entire field was lit up like Christmas. And since the eerie glow was there to stay for a while, McMinn decided to take advantage of the unnatural illumination to get some more plowing done.

"Seems like the old light felt real neighborly...and decided to help me with my plowing," McMinn told a reporter after the incident. "I couldn't see too well, and I guess the old light sensed it, because he started hovering all over the field where I was plowing."

That was fine until the strange light suddenly started acting funny. After about fifteen minutes of bobbing and weaving, casting strange shadows across the freshly-turned rows, it began to pulsate rhythmically. Long grainy fingers of incandescence clawed toward him, giving him plenty of light but also lots of goosebumps.

"I was absolutely frozen stiff to my tractor until it suddenly went away and vanished," he explained.

A few days earlier, in that same part of Oklahoma, a school bus full of children was nearly run off the road because of a menacing blue light perched on the rear window. Louise Graham, who was aboard the bus, said the children were terrified, thinking that the pesky light was trying to get in.

"The light was so bright that it temporarily blinded the driver," she said. "He had to stop the bus. Just as we stopped the light went away."

For years, thousands of Americans have encountered mysterious blue lights such as those described above. For some reason, the phenomenon seems to occur more frequently in Southern states—especially those with swamps and low-lying bogs and bayous.

No satisfactory theory has been advanced to account for these peculiar manifestations, known in most areas as "spooklights." Explanations range from the scientific to the fanciful, but perhaps the answer is somewhere in between.

The one constant thing about spooklights is that they never stay long, wherever they appear. They might last for only a few seconds or for half an hour, but they rarely last longer. There is some predictability about them—that is, some tend to show up at the same place at the same time, over and over, night after night, or at least to reappear in regular cycles.

In a tiny community near Joplin, Missouri, where the corners of Arkansas, Missouri, Oklahoma, and Kansas approach each other, one set of spooklights has been the subject of keen scientific inquiry for years. Spooksville, as the place is appropriately named, has also been a mecca for tourists hungry for supernatural adventure.

Not much is known about the Spooksville lights, except that they are among the most predictable anywhere. They have been seen by countless thousands of people from all walks of life. Hundreds of newspaper and magazine articles have been written about these unusual lights, and several feature film documentaries have appeared on television.

Some oldtimers believe the enigmatic nature of the lights has something to do with history. As it turns out, the area around Spooksville was once the preserve of the Cherokee Indians. Legend has it that the bobbing blue lights seen by busloads of tourists each year are the angry spirits of the Indians' ancestors, pulsing with incandescent fury at white men for their brutal and bloody treatment of Indians in years gone by.

Other folks suspect the lights might have something to do with the hundreds of innocent people who were slaughtered here during the Civil War. It was in this territory that "Border Ruffians" kept a reign of terror until the war ended in 1865. These "Ruffians" were nothing more than gangs of guerrilla troops working outside the frameworks of their respective armies to kill and rob and plunder remote areas of Missouri, Kansas, Arkansas, and other border states.

For a while, this territory was known as "Bleeding Kansas"—for the hundreds of men, women, and children who perished in the cruel fighting.

If you want to talk spooklights and history, go to the local museum. There you'll likely meet up with Mr. L.W. Robertson, the curator, who says he probably knows as much about the phenomenon as anyone else alive.

He also keeps an open mind on the subject.

"I have no idea what the spooklight is," Robertson says matter-of-factly. "And I've looked at it as much as any living man. I don't tell the tourists any story about the light at all. If they don't believe it, it's here for them to see for themselves."

Robertson's first experience with the phenomenon came shortly after World War II when he accompanied the U.S. Army Corps of Engineers into the area to investigate the lights. A few years before—during the war, in fact—reports about the ghostly goings-on at Spooksville had reached the highest levels of the Pentagon.

The Army High Command decided to investigate—just in case the phenomena had any military significance, Robertson explained.

"The Corps checked out the area for several miles, testing

caves, mineral deposits, and highway routes, and making aerial surveys," the curator noted. "They came to no conclusion."

In 1960, a student at Drury College in nearby Springfield decided to study the lights for himself and perhaps earn some extra academic credit in the process. For his project, Rob Gibbons, a freshman, chose one of the most haunted areas around: a narrow dirt road some eleven miles southwest of Joplin, near the Missouri-Oklahoma line.

Over the years, hundreds of reliable eyewitnesses had reported seeing the spooklights along the lonely road— usually appearing about dusk and continuing until the early hours of dawn. Accompanied by an assistant, Gibbons set up movie and still cameras, and settled back to await the arrival of the lights.

On February 24, 1965, he presented his conclusions at a student symposium in Springfield. Part of his discussion discounted the more fanciful accounts, pointing out that all his team had ever seen was a small light bobbing about at the end of the gravel road.

"Usually it seems to float over the hills down the roadway to the west," he remarked. "At rare times it seems to come towards the observer. At times it moves slightly horizontally. With a 30-power telescope...I could perceive as many as four distinct pairs of lights, with pairs of red lights appearing slightly to the right of pairs of bright white lights."

The red lights, he said, grew dimmer as the white lights became brighter.

Then Mr. Gibbons pulled out a map. While the silent audience looked and listened, the graduating student pointed out that U.S. Highway 66, running east and west between Quapaw and Commerce, was in direct line with the spooklight road and the observation point. Then he noted that the Spring River ran between the spooklight area and the highway, twelve miles away.

He added, "The phenomenon of the bright white lights appearing slightly to the left of the dimmer red lights corresponds with the natural movement of traffic on a road or highway."

As with all theories, skeptics were quick to denounce the student's new-fangled explanation of their beloved lights. The most glaring discrepancy, they charged, was that he had failed to take into consideration the fact that the spooklights had been around for a long, long time, predating the arrival of automobiles by almost a decade.

The first documented sighting of spooklights in the area was in 1903, almost a quarter of a century before Highway 66 was built.

The spooklights are still a mystery.

Secrets from Beyond the Grave

The Ghost That Came to Stay

One rainy night in the late 1920s, Mrs. Sammy King was sitting by an open window in her living room knitting a new shawl. She had just finished her second cup of tea and was about to start on her third when several jagged bolts of lightning crackled across the skies.

Mrs. King had always loved listening to and watching thunderstorms. As a child she had liked to run out and play in storms whenever her mother wasn't looking. Even as an adult she got a thrill out of watching dazzling displays of lightning followed by the booming peals of thunder.

But on this particular night, when Mrs. King was sixty-five, something told her this was no ordinary storm.

She suddenly felt afraid.

She shifted uncomfortably in the oversized armchair, mesmerized by the fierce beauty of the storm raging outside her window. Howling gusts of wind rocketed across the yard, rattling windows and doors and causing the long lace curtains by her head to flutter and pop. As the storm intensified, so did Mrs. King's fearfulness about it.

Finally, with the candles burning low, the elderly grandmother decided she'd better get up and shut the window, just to be safe. The second she started to rise, a blinding arrow of light slashed through the window and into Mrs. King's body, killing her on the spot.

Three days later her charred remains were taken to a small cemetery about two miles from her home in Dodge County, Georgia, and quietly laid to rest. But according to some locals, Mrs. King's spirit still haunts the property where she died so dramatically nearly seventy years ago.

Numerous eerie reports have surfaced over the years describing a "thin, stoop-shouldered" apparition wandering the fields and woods near the handsome old house near Eastman. The figure, always clad in dark colors and usually wearing an old-fashioned bonnet, has been seen picking flowers, gathering twigs and cones, and even sitting on the porch of her old house.

"She always wears a long brown dress with long sleeves and a scarf or bonnet that hides her face," said Betty Kight, who bought Mrs. King's property in 1962, "And she's usually surrounded by a soft haze of smoke."

Mrs. Kight, who never believed in ghosts before, said she first saw the specter shortly after she and her husband Bob moved in.

"I was in the kitchen putting things away when I looked through the window and saw this little old lady standing in the canna lilies. When I went outside, she was gone," she said.

After six such sightings—each lasting longer than the one before—Mrs. Kight said she got so afraid, she chopped down the canna lilies. That didn't stop the hauntings, however.

"It got worse," she said. "The ghost started visiting my children, even in broad daylight."

Although husband Bob has never actually seen the ghost, Mrs. Kight says her children—all of whom grew up in the house—have.

"One day my son Robert heard singing, so he went out on the porch. There sat Mrs. King in the swing with three children around her singing out of a song book," she explained.

There have been countless other encounters with the ghostly apparition, including one by daughter Elaine that still leaves Mrs. Kight's hair standing on end.

"One night after supper Elaine started out to feed the dogs. She opened the door with a plate of scraps in her hands, and there stood Mrs. King. Elaine screamed and threw the plate in the floor and slammed the door," Mrs. Kight said.

At first the Kights had no idea who—or what—the ghost was that haunted their property. Later, after talking with neighbors and relatives of the old house's former owners, they learned that their spectral visitor from beyond was none other than Mrs. Sammy King, a kind, gracious woman who had been struck by lightning and killed sometime in the late 1920s.

Descriptions of Mrs. King, said Mrs. Kight, matched that of her ghost from the top of her bonnet to the heels of her black, lace-up shoes.

Apparently members of the Kight family were only the latest in a growing list of people who claimed to have seen Mrs. King's ghost.

A decade of the haunting was enough for the Kights. In 1973, they built a new house about a hundred yards away from the old house and moved in, hoping such action might rid them of the unwanted presence. Two weeks after they settled in, however, more strange things started happening. Flickering lights were spotted in the window of the old woman's room across the way, and moaning, sobbing sounds were sometimes heard outside in the yard at night.

Then, almost imperceptibly, the silent ghost began to make its presence known in the new house. At first it was only the opening and closing of doors and moving things around that bothered the Kights. Soon, however, there were more sightings. So many, in fact, the Kights thought of bringing in an exorcist.

They never did.

Instead, the Kights began to grow fond of the kindly old presence that continues to fade in and out of view at unpredictable moments.

"We've just accepted the fact that she's here," explained Mrs. Kight matter-of-factly.

Now, instead of running or being afraid, the Kights consider the ghost part of the family.

"She's friendly, and she doesn't want to hurt us. I almost feel like she's part of our family."

In the beginning, the harassed family thought of selling

their haunted house and moving away—far away, so the ghost wouldn't follow. After a while, they changed their minds.

"I really think she's attached to us," Mrs. Kight said, adding that she believes the ghost of Mrs. King still haunts her property because "she didn't finish her mission here on earth."

Better Run When the
"Man in Gray" Comes Calling...

Early one morning in the autumn of 1954, an automobile dealer named Bill Collins looked out over the gray waves breaking in front of his beachfront house at Pawleys Island, South Carolina, and saw something strange.

Down on the beach, just a few yards from a gazebo Collins had built on a high sand dune, there stood a somber little man, fully clothed in a gray suit, and staring directly toward him. At first Collins, a practical man, didn't think much about the strangely dressed beachcomber. People walked up and down the beach all the time, and these days, some of them dressed pretty weird.

But there was something different about this unusual little fellow. The more Collins studied him, the more uncomfortable he felt. Was it the eyes? There seemed to be an odd glow in the stranger's eyes, a penetrating, faraway look that sent shivers down Collins's spine.

A deep sense of urgency seemed to radiate from the man, yet he stood unmoving, serene in a kind of otherworldly calmness.

Without understanding why, Collins was suddenly seized with the thought that the mysterious man in the gray suit down on the beach was trying to warn him about something. If so, then why didn't he speak up, and not just stand there gawking?

The thing that bothered Collins most was the peculiar

way in which the stranger was attired. The coat was cut long in the back in an old-fashioned style, and the tie and hat clearly belonged to another age. Perhaps there had been a masquerade party somewhere down the beach he didn't know about. Perhaps the man just liked to walk up and down the beach dressed funny.

Whatever, Collins finally decided he'd had enough mystery for one morning and started walking toward the stranger. He was sure there was a perfectly plausible explanation for the weird little man's dress, presence, and unfathomable behavior.

When he got within a few feet of him, however, Collins stopped dead in his tracks. While a pair of gulls shrieked overhead and the surf crashed on the beach, an unbelievable thing happened—the man in the gray suit started to fade! He was actually dissolving, like water poured onto a sandy beach, right before Collins' eyes.

Before Collins quite realized what was happening, the stranger had vanished from the beach.

At that moment, several hundred miles to the south, a major storm system was thrashing its way northward across the open Atlantic. Collins had no way of knowing that within a few days the hurricane would slam into the soft southern beach, pulverizing Pawleys Island and much of the unprotected Carolina coast.

A few heart-stopping seconds after the enigmatic stranger had disappeared, Collins put two and two together and realized what he had seen—surely it had been none other than South Carolina's legendary "man in gray," the phantom doomed to walk the beaches forever, warning people about approaching storms.

Not a man to take chances, Collins quickly gathered up his family and a few personal belongings and fled the island. A couple of days later, Hurricane Hazel thundered ashore, flattening thirty-foot sand dunes and washing away scores of handsome beachfront houses. Collins's own house was spared—indisputable proof that it had, indeed, been the man in gray who had come to warn him.

According to a popular legend along the Carolina coast, the man in gray sometimes appears days or hours before a terrible storm. Those fortunate enough to see him—and who heed his warning—will be spared and their property won't be damaged.

Even Collins, who believed in the legend, was stunned when he returned to the beach and found his house still standing.

"The TV antenna didn't even blow down," said Collins, whose story appeared in dozens of newspapers in the wake of Hazel's vicious onslaught.

Carolina's man in gray has been much talked about since its origins in the early 19th century. Even today, some superstitious, and some not-so-superstitious, beachfront property owners keep a keen eye out for him whenever winds rise and the threat of a storm is in the air.

Several times in the past century the mysterious man in gray has been known to appear right before a hurricane hit. The first account of such a manifestation was prior to the great gale of 1804. That was followed by two hurricanes in 1806, one of which blew down the lighthouse on North Island.

The most memorable, though, were the hurricanes of September 1822, October 1893, and October 1954. In each case, several people reportedly saw a strange little man dressed in gray clothes walking the stormy beach.

According to some sources, the legend can be traced back to about 1800, when a handsome young man on his way to see his fianceé on North Island was killed. Some accounts say his horse tripped and threw him into a pit of quicksand which he was unable to escape. Another version maintains he drowned at sea.

After his death, his young bride-to-be supposedly had a startling dream in which her fiance appeared to her, arms wet and cold, as if rising from some watery or slimy grave. She interpreted it as a warning of some kind, and when she told her father about it, he whisked her off to Charleston to see a doctor.

While they were away, a great storm blew in, destroying not only their plantation but many others on the island, including the home of Robert Francis Withers, a prominent rice planter.

Had it not been for the girl's dreams, she and her father would have been on the island and perished. A new legend was born.

Ever since, people living along the South Carolina coast have told of seeing a strange little man dressed in a gray suit just before a storm. Some people believe strongly in the legend and evacuate when they hear of such a sighting.

Gifts from Beyond the Grave

In life, Charlene Richard was an ordinary little girl who liked dolls and went to church every Sunday. It was only after her death thirty years ago that the twelve-year-old became widely known.

Today Charlene's name is a household word in southeastern Louisiana's Cajun country, where many folks believe the girl still lives—even after death—as an angel sent to earth to help heal the sick and lame and to perform other miracles.

In recent years, thousands of Charlene's Roman Catholic followers have rallied to make known their desire to have their local girl made a saint. That process could take decades, but in the meantime residents of Richard, Louisiana, have launched a campaign to make the world aware of Charlene's special gifts from beyond the grave.

On the night of August 11, 1989—Charlene's birthday—a crowd of about four thousand Catholics gathered at her grave at St. Edward's Church outside Richard to pay homage to their young candidate for sainthood. Those present that night sincerely believed in the departed girl's ability to reach beyond the walls of the spiritual world and touch the lives of those in the physical.

One such man was Paul Olivier.

"We had a child who was a year old and diagnosed as having cancer of the larynx," Olivier, a retired state policeman, told a wire service reporter. "The doctors said it was very rare, but it was a killer. They put her life span at three, four, five months at the most."

Then Olivier heard about Charlene.

At first he was skeptical. He was a deeply religious man, but he still didn't know what to think about miracles or prophets or divine intervention in earthly life. Desperate for help, however, Olivier took his sick daughter to the dead Cajun girl's grave.

"We asked her to help us," Olivier explained.

That was in 1970. Today Angela Olivier is a nineteen-year-old junior at the University of Southeastern Louisiana.

"I would say that is a sign of a miracle," her father said. "A prayer was answered."

Olivier's story is similar to hundreds of others that started cropping up shortly after Charlene's death. Talk of the girl's miraculous healing powers spread like wildfire through this ruggedly scenic region, and soon network television and national newspapers and magazines began to report on some of the more spectacular events.

Though many accounts were dismissed as hallucinations or hoaxes, a number of puzzling cases remain a mystery—except to those who believe.

Ten years ago, Lucy and Roger Courville's five-year-old daughter was diagnosed as having inoperable cancer. They had heard about Charlene, and along with hundreds of other faithful members of the flock, made a pilgrimage to Charlene's grave.

After a day of prayerful worship, the Courvilles went away. So did the cancer. Laurie Courville is now fifteen and continues to show signs of improvement.

"We think it was a miracle from Charlene," remarked a family member who says the healed girl's parents visit Charlene's grave often to thank her for saving their daughter's life.

The Reverend Floyd Calais is a man of the cloth who also believes in Charlene. A short while after her death, Calais was the chaplain at a state hospital in Lafayette, in the heart of Cajun country. For months he had been hoping for an opportunity to relocate to a small parish. When he heard about Charlene, he went to her grave and prayed she would inspire the bishop to reassign him.

He was soon appointed pastor of the church where the girl was buried, about one hundred fifty miles northwest of New Orleans.

"When I found out which church I had, the hair on the back of my neck stood on end," Calais, now sixty-two, said.

Today there is a box on Charlene's grave where visitors hoping for miracles can drop their petitions. A steady stream of visitors come and go, mainly curiosity seekers anxious for a glimpse of the famous grave, and at night a candle burns to light the way.

The grave itself is of simple construction, marked with a marble headstone and two elevated slabs. Even though she isn't convinced herself about her late daughter's miracles, Mary Alice Richard, Charlene's mother, still visits the grave nearly every day.

"Charlene was not a remarkable child," Mrs. Richard said. "She was full of life. She liked sports and was always busy with something. She went to church and said her rosary, but she was just a normal little girl."

The Rev. Joseph Brennan, pastor of St. Edward Church where Charlene is buried, said it was the girl's death that made her a saint.

"Charlene taught the world not how to live, but how to die," Brennan said. "Thirty years ago they didn't have the pain medicine they have now, and she died in excruciating pain but in perfect grace. She became great at that time."

Although the United States has produced only three saints, the diocese of Lafayette has begun the slow process of sainthood for Charlene. Local officials of the church are still involved with the first step of the canonization process—collecting sworn testimonies from people about how Charlene performed miracles on their behalf.

Based on the information collected, it will be up to the Vatican to determine whether Charlene is suitable for sainthood. Veneration would come first, then beatification, and finally canonization, according to Father Calais.

"That really doesn't matter. I'm sure that Charlene is a

saint," he said. "I'm sure she is in heaven."

For those who have seen the miracles, the canonization of Charlene is only a formality.

"For us she is already a saint," said Wilson Daigle, who credits Charlene's intercession with helping his wife recover from a mental illness. "We talk to her and she understands us."

The Portrait That Came to Life

Few hauntings in American history have aroused more speculation or raised more hackles than the series of eerie events
that happened at Haw Branch plantation near Amelia, Virginia.

Ghostly visitations, bloodcurdling screams in the night,
sinister birds, and macabre portraits that dripped blood are
just some of the spooky goings-on said to have plagued the
handsome old manor house since Civil War times. Unexplained disturbances continue to baffle the plantation's modern owners, though they have long since lost their fear.

"It's something we've learned to live with," said Gibson
McConnaughey, who along with her husband Cary bought
the estate in 1964, "but at times it does get frightening."

In antebellum days, Haw Branch Planation was the focal
point of a sprawling, 15,000-acre estate, complete with
numerous outbuildings, slave quarters, and even a dry moat.
After the War between the States the plantation fell into
disuse and ruin. Like hundreds of other once-proud plantations in the South, it was abandoned to weeds and vandals.

Nearly a hundred years later, in 1964, the McConnaugheys bought the property, which had once belonged to
Mrs. McConnaughey's grandmother. Mrs. McConnaughey
remembers playing in the house as a child, but for the past
fifty years or so, no member of the family had lived in the
house.

Restoration was tedious. Not only did the main house
with its tall brick chimneys and brooding columns undergo

massive rehabilitation, but acres of fields and rolling yards had to be cut back and preened. Finally, after four years of hard work, one of the South's most noted architectural gems was gleaming again.

Then the portrait arrived.

The subject was a beautiful young woman, said to be a distant and long-dead relative named Florence Wright. When the portrait was uncrated, the McConnaugheys were astonished to find a dingy black and white drawing rather than the brilliant pastel they were promised by the cousin who gave it to them as a housewarming gift.

Gibson McConnaughey dutifully hung the portrait over the library mantel anyway, thinking how much her ancestor would have appreciated it. Less than a month later, Mrs. McConnaughey made a startling discovery: either she was losing her mind, or the portrait was turning colors! In the light, certain parts of the canvas appeared to be bleeding.

Startled, she called in her husband and several visitors to see for themselves. Sure enough, over the next few weeks, fresh and living color began to creep into almost every gray and black tone in the picture.

It was as if the "dead" portrait had been brought back to life inside the old house!

Accompanying the eerie changes on the canvas were sounds—strange, bloodcurdling sounds, mostly that of a woman screaming from upstairs somewhere. The sounds continued on a regular basis for several years, coming usually at six-month intervals—on November 23 and May 23. The sounds were replaced by the apparition of a young woman, first seen by Mrs. McConnaughey in the summer of 1967.

"I could plainly see the silhouette of a slim girl in a floor-length dress with a full skirt," she was quoted as saying. "I could see no features, but she was not transparent, just a white silhouette. I saw her for perhaps ten seconds. In the next instant she was gone."

The bewildered Mrs. McConnaughey saw the ghost several times again, floating about the house in various rooms. Her daughter awoke once in the middle of the night to see a "lady in white" standing over her bed.

"Before I could say anything, the lady disappeared right in front of my eyes," the daughter said, noting that the presence had actually reached down and touched her.

On the night of May 23, 1968, the entire family sat up anticipating another visitation. They heard heavy footsteps thudding across the yard, but this time found nothing. Early the next morning, the McConnaughey children saw a giant bird standing in the yard in the moonlight under their windows.

"It was standing there with its wings spread out, appearing to have a wingspan of over six feet," Mrs. McConnaughey noted.

The bird was never seen again, but other curious things occurred in and around the old house. For example, the ghostly tinkling of cowbells was heard circling the house at night (there were no cows on the property); the scent of rosebuds and oranges lingered throughout the house at times (the family kept no fresh flowers in the house); and the McConnaugheys were awakened several times by what sounded like bodies falling into the dry moat.

On yet other occasions, some family members saw what looked like an old man carrying a kerosene lantern across the yard.

None of the strange events that happened at Haw Branch Plantation have ever been sufficiently explained to the McConnaughey family, who continue to reside in one of America's most famous haunted houses.

"Dead" Men Do Tell Tales

Frederick J. Harvey was only twenty years old—much too young to die. So thought his grief-stricken fiancee, Lily Godfrey, who insisted that her betrothed was only sleeping.

Even when the doctor came and pronounced the young man dead, even when the undertakers came and took him away, even after the corpse was walled up inside the family tomb three days later, Lily pleaded with family members to keep a constant vigil over the crypt, so obsessed was she that her beloved would soon awaken from a deep sleep and rush into her arms.

It took almost a week, but finally Lily's persistence paid off. Frederick's father, a wealthy Kansas restaurateur, agreed to re-open the tomb and take his dead son back home.

Lily was nearly overcome with joy!

Back home at the Harveys' palatial estate, young Frederick's body was dressed and put to bed. There he remained, still and ghastly white, beneath the silken covers of the four-poster bed for nearly four months.

In all that time, Lily Godfrey never once left her fiancee's side. She talked to him and sang to him, bathed him and even tried to feed him repeatedly. Every morning and every night she would kiss him on the forehead, hoping to detect warmth, some kind of vital sign.

Four long months passed.

Then, late one night when a stiff October wind rustled around the trees outside the window, an incredible thing happened.

Lily sat at the foot of the bed, staring into the crackling hearth, questioning her own sanity. The moon had risen high, casting a silvery glow over the satin sheets covering Frederick's still form. Suddenly Lily heard a groan. At first she thought it was the wind, scratching and moaning at the window.

When she heard it again, she spun toward the bed. There sat her would-be husband—limp, disheveled, and in obvious pain, but very much alive.

She could scarcely believe her eyes. What if this were a dream, a cruel hallucination?

Perhaps she had already gone mad.

She pinched herself, poked her arm with a pin.

Pain.

She closed her eyes, reopened them.

Frederick still sat there, only now he was moaning more loudly than before. He was also rubbing his head. His first words were, "Water...please."

For several long seconds Lily continued to stare at her "dead" fiance, listening to his deep breathing grow steadily more regular. Then, shivering like a leaf, she rose slowly from her chair and walked over to the bed.

"Frederick," she said, the words like taffy in her constricted throat.

She looked deep into the "corpse's" eyes. They were like dark pools clouded over with misty shadows.

"Lily," Frederick rasped, reaching for her.

Lily had time for one muffled scream before she dropped to the floor in a dead faint.

A few days later Frederick Harvey emerged completely from the trance that nearly cost him his life. Had Lily not insisted that he be brought back home—had he been left longer behind in that thick and musty tomb, he would have surely suffocated.

As it was, he recovered fully and married the woman who brought him back from the dead.

Frederick's grisly encounter with premature burial happened in 1906. In those days, mortuary science was still primitive at best, even though the practice itself had been around for countless thousands of years. In early America, as in many other countries, corpses were rarely embalmed. And since little was known about catalepsy, coma, and other such conditions, untold numbers of "dead" men and women no doubt went prematurely to their graves.

To awaken in a coffin beneath the ground or trapped in a tomb was a great fear of early Americans. No fate could be more horrid, no terror more crippling, than the realization that one had been buried alive. Such anxieties were often expressed in the literature and drama of the day, most notably in Edgar Allen Poe's "The Premature Burial."

Because top medical authorities considered the only sure sign of death to be "putrefactive decomposition," clauses in wills frequently required that bodies not be buried until a week after apparent death. "Waiting mortuaries" were once widely advocated; some were even built.

One sure-fire way to avoid the horrors of premature burial was to have one's remains cremated. In some European countries, it became customary to slit a corpse's jugular vein—just in case.

According to one story, 19th century writer Harriet Martineau went so far as to express in her will her wish to be decapitated upon death.

Eventually someone came up with a kind of "safety coffin." This contraption was designed to allow periodic viewing of the body from above ground, while at the same time provide a means of escape for a prematurely buried person.

"Safety coffins" and other specially-rigged devices for the grave were in hot demand in the late 19th century, when the news was full of premature burials. In 1862, Franz Vester patented a coffin containing an air tube and a bell, with a ladder to facilitate exit from the grave. In 1882 Albert Fearnaught began selling coffins in which the slightest movement from within would make a flag wave above the tombstone.

One remarkable "safety-oriented" coffin was put on the market in 1903. Emily Josephine Jephson described her invention thus: "Jephson's improved Coffin for indicating the burial alive of a person in a trance or suffering from a comatose state so that same may be released or rescued, has means for admitting air to the coffin and for giving an audible signal by means of an electric bell, which may be placed either on the grave or in the cemetery house.

"There is a glass plate in the lid, and a small shelf attached to one side of the coffin which may hold a hammer, matches, and candle so that, when the person wakes, he can light the candle and with the hammer break the glass, thus assisting to liberate himself when the earth...in removed."

Other patents were equally ingenious.

In 1906 J. J. Toolen put together a contraption utilizing a battery-operated spring lid that would power a light for one hundred fifty hours. Another inventor suggested chaining the body to a spring-loaded lid on a coffin buried in shallow earth. Should the unfortunate victim inside return to life and make the slightest movement, the lid would yank open and he or she could literally walk away from the grave.

It wasn't until after World War I that advances in forensic medicine began to lessen fears about premature burial. As the certification of death became a more accurate science, fewer people feared going to their graves while they yet lived.

*Gold, Shrines
and Ancient Stones*

Bedford County's "Lost" Treasure

At first glance, Bedford County, Virginia, might seem like an unlikely place to go treasure hunting.

With its gently sloping hills and quiet rural lifestyle, this corner of the Cavalier State seems more suited to fox hunting and relaxed strolls down secluded country lanes than to digging for buried gold and silver.

For the past decade or so, thousands of people from all across the country have been coming here to do just that. Armed with computerized mapping systems, electronic scanning devices, and a vast array of other sophisticated equipment, these modern-day treasure hunters are leaving no stone unturned in their quest to find the spot where a legendary fortune in gold and silver is supposed to be buried.

It all began more than one hundred sixty years ago when an eccentric old Virginian named Thomas J. Beal went west to seek his fortune. The hometown folk had laughed at him when he told them his plans, but one day he sold his cabin, loaded up his wagon, and drove away without saying goodby to a soul.

After years of mining the rugged backcountry of New Mexico, the old miner was about to give up when late one afternoon he happened to spot something glittering at the back of a cave. Curious, he pushed his way closer through the dust and gloom. Leaning over, he peered at the strange piece of rock jutting from the wall.

There, in the silence of that old cave hundreds of miles from his hometown in Virginia, the old man's heart nearly gave way.

In the dim light he could see it clearly now. Gold! Tons and tons of it, beautiful and gleaming, whole veins of it, stretching back into the cave as far as he could see.

At long last, Beal had struck it rich.

Sometime toward the end of the following year—1821—the lucky miner loaded up several wagons with his glittering fortune and casually drove back to Virginia. Aboard the wagons was his entire fortune—$21 million in gold and silver, stripped from the thirty mines he had worked in New Mexico.

Back home in Bedford County, the first thing Beal did was hide his treasure—wagons and all. Some of the precious lode he concealed in iron pots, which he carefully buried beneath the wagons. Then, for reasons which remain unknown, the curious multi-millionaire pulled up roots and headed back out to New Mexico. He was never seen or heard from again, but before departing, he did leave behind some enigmatic instructions about how to find the lost treasure.

It is those instructions, set out in a kind of secret code, that many seekers of the fortune have been using to try to find Beal's elusive booty. Those who believe in the legend say it's only a matter of time before some lucky hunter unravels the mysterious clues.

"It's down there somewhere, and one day somebody's going to find it," said Eddy Toner, who, along with his brother Joe, has spent the past nine years probing for the treasure. " I get shaky just thinking about it."

The Toner brothers are among scores of "serious" searchers who swarm into rural Bedford County periodically to dig, sift, and poke. Many, like Wilbur Swift of Garden Grove, California, have given up regular jobs and invested their life savings in the project.

"Several times I've come close, so close," Swift, a former computer programmer, explained in an interview, "I'm going to keep digging until I find it."

As for those who don't understand, or who laugh at his quest, Swift has this to say: "He who laughs last, laughs best. I believe I'll have the last laugh."

Ken Dooley, a local contractor, has made a lot of money renting out his equipment to outsiders interested in finding the treasure. Although he tends to doubt the veracity of the legend himself, he figures that as long as other people believe in it, he'll keep supplying them with the tools they need to look for it.

"Everybody who comes in here is always excited," Dooley said. "They're always about two feet away from striking it rich."

Diggers come and diggers go, but so far the secret of Beal's treasure remains just that—a secret. Was it all just a hoax? Did Beal, about whom very little is known today, concoct the story as a joke? Or was he merely seeking revenge against the people who had laughed at him when he told them he was going out west to find his fortune.

Chances are we'll never know the truth. One thing seems sure, though—as long as there remains a shred of possibility the treasure might be for real, the hills and woods of Bedford County will get no rest.

Romancing the Stones of Georgia

High atop a windswept meadow in the rural hills of north Georgia stands a mysterious assembly of granite stones that has intrigued locals and baffled visitors from around the world since its construction almost a decade ago.

The stones, which bear a remarkable resemblance to England's Stonehenge and stand at the mythological center of the Cherokee Indians' world, are said to possess occult powers, while offering guidance for preserving a threatened civilization—or rebuilding a destroyed one.

Known as the Georgia Guidestones, the megalithic structure was built and paid for in 1980 by an unknown benefactor under the assumed name of Robert C. Christian.

Christian's true identity, like the origins and purpose of the Guidestones, remains shrouded in mystery, the subject of considerable controversy in the small Georgia town of Elberton, which bills itself as the "granite capital of the world."

According to William A. Kelly, executive vice president of the Elberton Granite Association, Inc., who oversees much of Elberton's internationally famous granite production, the Guidestones are among the most unusual man-made monuments in North America.

"Not only is its massive size larger than any other single monument manufactured in these parts, the circumstances surrounding its origin, completion and erection have undoubtedly caused more speculation and comment than any of the other millions of granite memorials...since the area's famed granite industry started nearly a century ago."

The configuration of stones, which rises more than nineteen feet above a grassy knoll overlooking Georgia Highway 77, consists of four major columns that radiate like giant symmetrical tablets with a slimmer stone in the center and another capping the top of the structure. Etched into the towering stones are ten messages, or "commandments," translated into twelve languages, including English, Russian, Arabic, Sanskrit, Babylonian cuneiform, Egyptian hieroglyphics, and classical Greek.

Each year, thousands of curiosity-seekers from as far away as Europe and Canada visit the Guidestones. Among the visitors are self-styled witches and warlocks who claim the stones project an energy force because of their unique astronomical alignment with solar and celestial movements and summer and winter solstices.

According to Naunie Batchelder, who teaches at the Foundation of Truth in Atlanta, Elbert County has a very high form of energy, a "special energy some would call a vortex or power spot. We don't know exactly where, but it's here on this hill."

Former Elberton mayor Joe Fendley acknowledges that the monument had become the center of a kind of "occult-type" activity.

"There have been some occult-type things going on out there, also tribal ritualistic dancing, and nude dancing," he told a newspaper. "But there have also been Christian activities there and even a wedding."

Adding to the mystical aura of the stones is a historical marker nearby designating the site as the center of the world.

"This was Al-yeh-li A lo-Hee, the center of the world to the Cherokee Indians," the inscription on the marker reads. "To this assembly ground from which trails radiate in many directions, they came to hold their councils, to dance and worship, which to them were related functions."

Elberton's reputation as the so-called "granite capital of the world" was instrumental in attracting the mysterious Mr. Christian in the first place, according to Hudson Cone, who works for the Elberton Granite Association.

"About all we know is that late one afternoon this fellow walked into the offices of the Elberton Granite Finishing Company and said he wanted to buy a monument—a very large monument," Cone explained. "The man, who identified himself as a Christian gentleman concerned with the welfare of humanity, said he wanted the monument to be about twenty feet high, and it was designed to spread a message to mankind."

Pyramid blue granite was chosen for the project, and soon construction began on what Cone described as "an almost impossible task." During excavation of the site, and later on during construction, several workers reported hearing strange sounds echoing across the lonely hills. Some workers complained of dizziness and light-headedness at times.

Because of the massive size of the stones, each weighing about twenty-eight tons, special equipment had to be brought in to lift the stones from their resting places one hundred fourteen feet inside the quarry. Key craftsmen and special crews were called in to assist with the project, which took more than nine months to complete.

Today the enigmatic stone assembly continues to intrigue locals as well as outsiders. No one knows how many visitors have been drawn to the ring of Guidestones over the years, but one local county official estimates it in the tens of thousands.

As the mystery of Georgia's bizarre circle of stones grows deeper, so do the myths that surround its origin and meaning. It is likely that the true meaning and purpose behind the silent ring of Georgia stones will remain locked within the realm of myth forever.

The End of Jefferson, Texas

On the eve of the American Civil War, a number of former frontier towns in east Texas seemed on the verge of being called the next great western city.

One of those towns was Jefferson, a sprawling riverfront community of thirty thousand inhabitants nestled in the northeast corner of the state not far from Shreveport, Louisiana. With its bustling cotton economy and easy access to the Mississippi River, there was every reason to believe that Jefferson, would soon overtake Houston or even Dallas as the premier commercial center of the Lone Star State.

By 1860 newspapers from Boston to San Francisco were hailing Jefferson as the "Queen of the West." All day long and into the warm southern nights, flotillas of packet boats, piled high with bales of cotton, steamed down Big Cypress River on their way to market.

On any day of the week, there were twelve to fifteen steamboats lined up along the three-mile waterfront, bells ringing and whistles blowing. A favorite pastime among the citizenry was to gather along the docks to watch the colorful boats arrive, unload their goods, and then depart amid billowing clouds of smoke and fire.

Some of the wealthiest folks in Texas—planters, gamblers, cattlemen—traveled these steamers where multi-million-dollar deals were often signed over card tables or in the comfortable, smoke-filled salons of the upper decks. This was definitely the antebellum fast lane, and a trip up or down the winding river aboard one of the handsomely appointed showboats was considered a significant social event in the region.

If you happened to be born into the right social circumstances, the mid-19th century was, indeed, a glorious time to be alive in Old Jefferson. Ladies and gentlemen of standing, clad in hoop skirts, bonnets, and tailcoats, frolicked on the lawns of their gracious homes, while up-and-coming entrepreneurs, planters, and other young fortune hunters plotted their social and financial destinies along the bustling, cotton-laden waterfront.

There was even talk of a railroad coming to town. Leading businessmen, keenly aware of the financial benefits to be gained from completion of a new rail line, had visions of vast wealth flowing into their once obscure little corner of the South.

Even though the winds of war were beginning to blow across the young nation, few Jeffersonians had reason to suspect their good fortune would ever come to an end. Life was simply too wonderful to imagine that it could ever change.

Chances are that Jefferson's future would have remained as bright as the Texas sun had it not been for the intervention of one man.

By the late 1850s, Jay Gould was one of the most powerful—if not most respected—men in the nation. A self-made millionaire by the time he was twenty-one, Gould's life story had followed the classic rags-to-riches pathway to success. As a teenager, he had entered the leather trade, working his way to the top, and then gone on to Wall Street, where he became one of the world's savviest financiers.

As a further measure of Gould's unquestioned ability to make money, he quickly put together a second fortune after having lost everything in the Panic of 1857. After the South's surrender at Appomattox, Gould emerged as one of the most ruthless land speculators of the century. He also started buying and selling railroads much the same way other men did stocks and bonds.

It was no secret that Jay Gould's determination to succeed

led him to dabble in a series of unscrupulous business ventures involving bribery, stock market fraud, and judicial injunctions. According to his own biographers, Gould's attempts at cornering the nation's gold supply on Black Friday 1869 was the most notorious maneuver in a long and shady career.

In the 1870s Gould turned speculator again, this time targeting rapidly expanding western railroads such as the Union Pacific. Still only in his forties, Gould juggled control of a dozen new lines; by 1890 he reportedly owned half the railroad mileage in the Southwest. Across the dusty plains and deserts they went, hundreds of miles of gleaming new track finally linking the eastern and western halves of the growing nation.

But when Jay Gould came to Texas demanding concessions for his new line, the citizens of Jefferson shook their proud heads. Instead of bowing down before the undisputed king of the railroads, Jeffersonians appeared content to allow commerce to continue as it had before, along the muddy waters of Big Cypress River.

Besides, nobody wanted the clang and smoke of dirty locomotives lumbering through the streets of their clean, tranquil city. Residents of the "Queen of the West" were protective of their tree-lined avenues, handsome frame shops and houses, and landscaped parks.

When Gould failed to get his way, he left in a huff, taking his railroad with him three miles away. Before leaving, however, the wizard of Wall Street paused long enough to put a curse on Jefferson. The curse, written down on the register of the hotel where he had stayed, was a chilling prediction that Jefferson would soon dry up and blow away like a Texas tumbleweed.

"It's the end of Jefferson, Texas," he wrote. "Grass will grow in your streets and bats will roost in your belfries if you do not let me run my railroad through your town."

Jeffersonians scoffed at the strange warning—but not for long. Just up the river, near Shreveport, the federal government had already started dredge work on the Big Cypress.

Almost overnight the once-mighty river was reduced to a mere trickle; now, with no water route, cotton bales stood rotting along abandoned waterfront docks.

Within months of his departure, Gould's eerie prediction had come true. As the river dried up, so did the town. Jefferson sank into a period of decay from which it wouldn't emerge for years. Grass and weeds soon choked the streets and the fluttering wings of bats could be heard in the deserted attics and belfries of Jefferson.

Ancient Footprints in Stone

Most anthropologists agree that mankind originated in Africa at some remote time in the past, and then migrated to the New World across a now-submerged Asian landbridge about 25,000 years ago.

But hold on.

If that theory is true, what on earth are human footprints doing buried on a Kentucky farm in sediment laid down at least 250 million years ago?

How can it be that workers digging along the Mississippi River once uncovered a slab of sandstone containing a pair of fossilized "humanoid" tracks supposedly millions of years old?

Clearly, if these ancient footprints in stone are genuine, something must be wrong with our fossil record. Otherwise, how is it possible that man-like creatures roamed North America millions of years before the emergence of *Australopithecus* in Africa and Asia?

These are only some of the troubling questions being raised in light of several new and not-so-new findings in paleontology, the branch of geology that deals with prehistoric plant and animal fossils. What is slowly emerging is not only the startling possibility that mankind has flourished in the New World for millions of years, but also the astounding proposition that he perhaps walked North America during the time of the dinosaurs.

One of the most compelling bits of evidence attesting to man's antiquity in the New World was found in a dry river bed near Glen Rose, Texas, about sixty years ago. Residents happened to notice that each time the Paluxy River dried up, giant man-like footprints, some measuring eighteen inches long and five to seven inches wide, would show up adjacent to those of dinosaur tracks—irrefutable proof, said some, that forerunners of man had lived during the age of the great reptiles.

In one striking discovery, for example, the footprints of a man-like creature actually overlapped that of a three-toed dinosaur—a creature that paleontologists insist became extinct more than sixty-six million years ago!

Quick to cash in on the quirky find, some locals began digging up tracks and hawking them to tourists. It's no secret, of course, that large numbers of these "tracks" were fakes sold to gullible customers. But a lot of people who profited from the business testified their tracks were authentic.

Jim Ryals was one such man. In sworn testimony, he admitted that he and his wife sold tracks to tourists, but that some were the real thing. Ryals reportedly told investigators that he and his wife had removed several of the prehistoric human tracks from the Paluxy riverbed, using a chisel and a sledgehammer.

According to Ryals, there was a way that real prints could be distinguished from fakes:

"First, the pressure of the foot usually pushed up a ridge of mud around the outside of the track. Second, if the track is broken open or sawed, pressure lines can be found beneath the surface...

"Furthermore...when the (real) tracks were chiseled out of the riverbed, the workman was usually very careful to do his chiseling a good distance from the track for fear of damaging it. This resulted in a rather wide circle of the limestone surrounding the footprint."

It was common knowledge that local hucksters involved in the lucrative track trade knew the difference between real ones and fakes—that is, they were able to fashion their own versions by carefully copying the authentic models in the riverbed. Some became so skilled at their craft it was difficult for even trained scientists to tell the real from the phonies.

Understandably, most scientists are reluctant to even consider the authenticity of the Glen Rose tracks since dinosaurs supposedly died off millions of years before the evolution of *Homo sapiens* from small, warm-blooded creatures. Others who have looked at the evidence aren't so sure.

In 1976, Jack Walper, a professor of geology at Texas Christian University, conducted studies that offered additional proof that the human prints were genuine. In a series of tests, he showed that the pressure of each fossilized footfall had forced the mud upward—indicating that actual human beings had made the prints at some time in the past contemporary with dinosaurs.

The truth behind the Glen Rose tracks remains a mystery, as do some other startling finds linking man to prehistoric times. Shortly before the outbreak of World War I, for example, Dr. Wilbur Burroughs, head of the geology department of Berea College in Kentucky, discovered what he called "humanoid" footprints in carboniferous sandstone on a farm belonging to O. Finnel in the hills of Rockcastle County, Kentucky.

Special tests on the Rockcastle tracks revealed no signs of carving or artificial marking in or around the prints—suggesting, of course, that the prints were authentic. The prints—found in rock estimated to be more than 250 million years old—were later destroyed by vandals.

During the War of 1812, noted American ethnologist Henry R. Schoolcraft excavated a pair of human footprints from a quarry along the Mississippi River near St. Louis. Schoolcraft, who found the tracks in a limestone deposit estimated to be 270 million years old, described them as "strikingly natural, exhibiting every muscular impression, and swell of the heel and toes, with a precision and faithfulness to nature, which I have not been able to copy, with perfect exactness..."

For years, some anthropologists have argued that the traditionally accepted timeframe of man's arrival in the New World is no longer satisfactory. A few, like Jeffrey Goodman, an engineering archaeologist from Tucson, Arizona, believe that man first developed in North America, then migrated westward toward Asia and the Old World.

Goodman bases his theory on "many individual bits and pieces of information in the archaeological record which, taken together, serve to fingerprint and document specific migrations in reverse...Based on the evidence now coming to light, I believe that there was migration in reverse. Instead of nomadic hunters coming from the Old World to populate the New World, I believe the Paleo-Indians from the New World, the first fully modern men anywhere in the world, traveled to the Old World and woke it from its sound evolutionary sleep."

Neither Goodman nor any of the other "America first" theorists can adequately account for the enigmatic presence of human footprints in stone deposits believed to be many millions of years old. These timeless tracks in stone remain one of the greatest mysteries of our time.

Improbable Encounters

The Galveston Sea Monster

The late afternoon sun hung low and hazy over the glassy waters of the Gulf of Mexico. Only the slightest of breezes stirred as the *Saint Olaf,* a Norwegian-registered bark with twenty-man crew, sailed slowly toward the port city of Galveston, Texas.

The voyage down from Newport had been slow and uneventful. Now, Captain Alfred Hassel, master of the small tri-masted vessel, and his sea-weary crew were looking forward to a few days of rest and relaxation on the warm Texas coast before sailing back to their cold, mist-shrouded homeland in Norway.

Hassel and the brave men of the *Saint Olaf* didn't suspect they were only minutes away from a terrifying encounter with the unknown. Less than a few hundred yards ahead, not yet visible in the sparkling green waters, a long, sinuous shadow was undulating toward them. Soon the mariners would come face-to-face with their worst nightmare—a gigantic sea serpent.

The bizarre confrontation would make headlines around the world as reporters and scientists from New York to Paris flocked to Galveston to interview the captain and crew of the *Saint Olaf.* In his official public report, released two months after the incident, Hassel would provide a detailed account of the large "sea monster" that chased and threatened his ship that warm summer day in 1872.

All was going well until about 4:30 when Hassel, in his cabin studying tide charts, was summoned on deck by a

131

frantic sailor. The date was May 13, 1872. The *Saint Olaf* was less than two days from Galveston.

After putting away the charts and throwing on his cap, Hassel trudged up the steep flight of steps to go topside. He paused briefly for his eyes to adjust to the harsh glare of the setting sun, then strolled briskly over to the weather bow to see what all the commotion was about.

He had never seen his men so excited. Groups of sailors were leaning over the railing, pointing and shouting at some object far out at sea. A couple of seamen had scampered up the rigging, apparently to get a better view.

Hassel pushed his way past his men toward the railing.

"Over here, sir!" his first mate shouted. "You won't believe it."

The first thing the captain saw was a shoal of large sharks slicing quickly toward the boat. Within seconds their fins had disappeared beneath the hull, only to re-emerge moments later on the other side. Soon they had disappeared on the horizon. Hassel, a grizzled maritime veteran, had never seen such strange shark behavior. Apparently something was chasing them—something huge.

Then he saw it, rising over the shimmering, fire-tipped surface of the sea. At first, as it lurched toward them, the image was that of a bewhiskered old man tottering across the waves. But as it drew nearer, Hassel and every man on deck realized it wasn't like anything they had ever seen. In fact, they could now see it was some kind of creature—a hideous, evil-looking serpentine monster with horn and fins and a long, pointed tail.

Never had the men aboard the *Saint Olaf* seen such a dreadful sight. Some shrank away from the railing in fright; others made the sign of the cross. Even in their horror, however, not a single sailor dared take his eyes off the devil-sent behemoth slicing through the sea toward them.

Hassel was reminded of old pictures he had seen of the dreaded Kraken—the fabled deep-sea creature that was said to roam the open seas in search of wayward ships and their crews. Even in the Gulf there were stories of equally fearsome beasts that had attacked ships and devoured crewmen. But Hassel didn't believe in such fairy tales—until today.

Hassel's official statement, signed and released the following August, gave the following description of the strange apparition:

"On a nearer approach we saw that it was an immense serpent, with its head out of the water...about 200 feet from the vessel. He (the serpent) lay still on the surface (at first)...lifting his head up, and moving the body in a serpentine manner. Could not see all of it; but what we could see, from the after part of the head, was about 70 feet long and of the same thickness all the way, excepting about the head and neck, which were smaller, and the former flat, like the head of a serpent..."

Hassel said the creature had "four fins on the back, and the body of a yellow greenish color, with brown spots all over the upper part and underneath white."

In his sworn statement, Hassel also said the creature was about six feet in diameter, and that the waves "pushed out loudly" from its undulating motion.

The men of the *Saint Olaf* watched the creature for a full ten minutes before it finally sank beneath the waves and disappeared. One sailor thought he saw it resurface some time later, but no one was sure. The Galveston monster had simply vanished, like so many others reportedly spotted in the vicinity over the years.

Skeptics were quick to dismiss the sighting as nothing more than a long string of seaweed. In the fading afternoon sunlight, they reasoned, floating strands of weed rising and falling with the action of the waves could have easily been mistaken for a giant serpent. Others suspected the "creature" might have been a school of porpoises in pursuit of the rapidly-fleeing sharks.

Some experts theorized it might have indeed been a serpent—a giant boa constrictor or some other kind of large snake that had perhaps drifted across the Gulf from Central America. But seventy feet long? The longest known serpent in the New World—the anaconda—rarely exceeds twenty feet in length.

It is also doubtful that any kind of land snake could have survived such a long voyage across the shark-infested Gulf.

Through it all, the men of the *Saint Olaf* held fast to their story. They had seen a sea serpent—and lived to tell the tale.

Swarms of "Killer Bees" Will Soon Invade U.S.

For the past couple of decades, Americans living along the Mexican border have been gearing up for an invasion. When it comes, no wall will be high enough nor will any Star Wars defense shield be strong enough to keep out this airborne enemy.

Swarms of African bees, dubbed "killer" bees by the news media because their powerful stings have already resulted in the deaths of hundreds of human beings, are reportedly massing less than four hundred miles south of the Texas border for the big northern offensive. Moving at a rate of about three hundred miles a year, the bees were expected to reach the Brownsville area in March 1990. By 1993 they should reach Arizona, and California one year later.

Over the next several decades, the bees' relentless advance could take them as far north as Canada, provided their own defense systems are capable of adjusting to the colder climes.

What sounds like the ideal plot for a grade B science-fiction movie is being taken seriously by teams of scientists from Mexico City to Washington, D.C., who have been busy monitoring the progress of the bees for the past couple of decades. Some of the methods being considered to halt the relentless spread of bees sound like science fiction, as well— chemically-scented lures, solar-powered, infrared bee back-packs and a computerized noisemaker called a "Buzz Buster."

135

So far nothing seems to be working. About the only thing Americans can do is watch and wait while hundreds of swarms of vicious, mutant killer bees wing their way steadily northward.

Not much is known about the African bees since about thirty swarms were accidentally released in a Brazilian laboratory in 1956—except that they are extremely active, aggressive, and dangerous. At least four hundred people and thousands of animals have been killed by this highly excitable insect that attacks its victims en masse, stinging them to death with its powerful venom.

After their escape into the Brazilian jungle, these swarms of savage bees quickly crossbred with native varieties. The African bees, along with their "Africanized" cousins, then gradually spread through South and Central America into Mexico, terrorizing farmers and villagers along their 3,000-mile journey through ten countries.

In recent years, books, movies, and television shows have appeared predicting grim encounters between humans and large swarms of killer bees. Although scientists and professional beekeepers downplay such scenarios, the genetic makeup and ferocious behavior of the African bees could make them formidable foes in certain real-life situations.

One scientist said she had to "run for her life" several times when attacked by swarms of bees she was studying in Venezuela. Anita Collins of the U.S. Department of Agriculture said her primary motivation now for finding a way to stop or control bees stems directly from those attacks.

"I reached the point where I wanted to say something besides, 'Run like hell,'" she told a reporter.

Several swarms of bees have already reportedly reached south Florida. In 1988, about ten thousand bees were found at Fort Lauderdale aboard a freighter carrying fruit and vegetables from Guatemala. The bees had to be destroyed, as did the most recent swarm of five hundred found last year aboard a tanker in Miami.

Although the Florida swarms caught officials by surprise, the Agriculture Department, in anticipation of accidental bee arrivals, had set up several "bait hives" in the southern part of the state.

"The first bait hive we ever placed was in Miami because it's an area we've always been concerned about," said Agriculture Commissioner Doyle Conner. "There is just a tremendous interchange between Miami and Central and South American countries, virtually all of which are now infested with Africanized bees."

Florida now monitors about three hundred bait hives set up in thirteen port areas.

Beekeepers and scientists have long known that key genetic and behavioral differences existed between African bees and their tamer, gentler cousins in North America, but have only recently come to understand some of them. Killer bees, for example, tend to appear much more defensive around hives, aggressively assaulting and often pursuing for miles people or animals who come near.

For years scientists assumed that mating African bees with the gentler variety would cause them to lose their propensity to sting in potentially deadly swarms. But recent research has shown that the dilution of Africanized genes appears only to be temporary and that the bees' genetic makeup eventually becomes almost purely Africanized again, as is evident in wild swarms spreading up through Central America and southeastern Mexico.

"This African population is going to reach the U.S. virtually unchanged," said Orley Taylor, a University of Kansas insect ecologist.

Aside from the obvious physical danger, officials are haunted by other concerns brought on by the wild African bee invasion. For example, some scientists fear the bees will disrupt the nation's $200 million honey industry as well as damage $20 billion worth of pollinated field crops.

That's because African bees reproduce many times faster than domestic bees and tend to wreak havoc on less hostile honeybee colonies. At the same time, killer bees are known to be poor pollinators because of the drone's reputation as being a big consumer of honey.

In the past, the United States has withstood numerous menacing invasions from the south. This may be the first time our armies won't be able to defend us.

Where Did All the Dinosaurs Go?

Every school child knows that millions of years before the emergence of man, huge creatures called dinosaurs ruled the earth.

Thanks to the work of paleontologists, we not only know what these ancient animals looked like, we also know what they ate, how they reproduced, and where and when they lived.

What isn't so clear, however, is the fate that suddenly befell these beasts that once held sway over so much of our young planet and its shallow seas. Geologically speaking, the dinosaurs vanished in the twinkling of an eye.

The cause of their enigmatic passing is one of the greatest mysteries of all time.

Many theories have been advanced over the years to account for the extinction of the dinosaurs. New evidence coming forth from the ground in the Southeastern United States, however, links the end of the dinosaurs to a prehistoric global upheaval precipitated by the crash of a meteor or swarm of meteors about sixty-six million years ago.

Although this "impact theory" has many detractors, more and more scientists now accept the possibility that at some remote time in the past, a gigantic celestial object struck the earth, setting off a chain of climatic events that ultimately led to the demise of the dinosaurs.

If the theory holds up, it wouldn't be the first time that life forms on earth have been destroyed by death-dealing agents from beyond the solar system. According to some scientists, the fossil record is replete with evidence suggesting periodic mass extinctions. Exactly how and when they occurred, however, is a matter of unprecedented debate.

"These are exciting times to be looking at extinction," says Bevan French, a geologist with NASA.

Two schools of thought have emerged among extinction specialists. The first holds that mass extinctions on earth are somehow triggered by brief cataclysmic events such as the impact of a celestial body; others argue that the extinction process is gradual, brought on by environmental changes wrought by tectonic, oceanic, and climatic fluctuations.

When geologists and paleontologists look for evidence to support their theories, they usually turn to the fossil record left in rocks.

In Texas, scientists from Baylor University and Western Washington University have found what they believe are strong clues to support the impact theory—that is, that some large object from space, probably an asteroid or a comet, slammed into the western Atlantic Ocean approximately 66.4 million years ago, triggering a global catastrophe that ultimately killed off large animals on earth and in the sea. Their findings support that of other geologists working in Alabama, Arkansas, and off the Carolina coast.

Geologists Thor A. Hansen and O.T. Howard say the crash resulted in an ocean wave at least fifteen stories high that roared across shallow seas in east-central Texas. To support their claim, they point to a series of rock outcrops near the Brazos River southeast of Waco that still bear scars from that event millions of years ago.

"We calculated how much energy was necessary to rip up the kind of chunks of ocean floor that we found and then calculated the size of the wave," Hansen told reporters. He added that he believes the tsunami, or seismic sea wave, was more than fifty meters (about one hundred sixty feet) high.

Studies of rock formations elsewhere in the Southeast suggest "some sort of high-energy event" occurred about the same time, probably resulting from an impact somewhere in the Atlantic.

"We think we've proven there was a tsunami," Hansen noted. "We speculate that the wave was generated by some sort of extraterrestrial impact."

Such a celestial impact could have resulted in a scenario straight out of a science-fiction movie: giant meteor slams into the earth, kicking up enormous clouds of dust and smoke from blazing volcanoes. Other volcanoes erupt, tidal waves surge across landscapes, and the skies grow dark for months, perhaps years.

Unable to adjust to the altered environmental conditions, countless species are wiped off the face of the planet. Dinosaurs—cold-blooded, many of them quite large—are biologically less flexible, and perish in great numbers. Smaller creatures—especially tiny, fur-clad, warm-blooded mammals—escape to continue their evolution.

At least that is the picture being painted by some advocates of the impact theory. Such a view would have been considered radical until about a decade ago when scientists found large amounts of iridium layered in deposits made about the time the dinosaurs became extinct. Iridium is a rare metal on earth but common in meteorites.

These and other recent findings continue to shed light on the fate of our ancient forerunners and may contain clues to our own uncertain future.

Florida's "Watcher in the Woods"

The Fort Lauderdale, Florida, police department was accustomed to receiving strange calls in the middle of the night, but nothing had prepared them for the unusual message they received on the morning of January 9, 1974.

A young man who identified himself as Richard Lee Smith said he had run over a "giant black man" on Hollywood Boulevard, a busy area even at four o'clock in the morning.

"Is he dead?" the dispatcher wanted to know.

"I think so," Smith replied in a trembling voice. "But he's gone."

"You mean he's a goner?" the dispatcher asked.

"No, I mean he's dead, but he's gone," Smith answered.

Then Smith assured the officer this was no crank call—nor was it just any ordinary traffic accident involving a pedestrian.

"Please send someone out here," he pleaded. "Hurry!"

An officer named Johnson was immediately dispatched to the scene. Smith was waiting for him, huddled inside his locked car. When the officer arrived, the young man slowly got out.

Smith explained what happened.

He had been travelling at about fifty miles an hour when a huge man wearing what appeared to be dark clothing suddenly stepped out in front of him. He swerved to avoid hitting the man, but instead of stepping away from the car, the pedestrian bolted directly into its path.

Smith said he felt—and heard—the sickening crunch of

his front right wheel rolling over bones. Afraid he had killed the man, Smith stopped the car, got out, and ran back to examine the victim.

That's when he nearly died of fright.

In a state of shock, he watched a large, hairy "creature-like thing" rise slowly off the pavement. Even in the dim glow of the street lamp, Smith could clearly see what he had hit. The "thing" stood well over eight feet tall, he said, and made a roaring sound. Then it made a move toward him.

"That's when I jumped in the car and took off," Smith told the officer.

Johnson, not overly impressed by the young man's wild story, dutifully looked over the car's damaged front end. The front had bloodstains, to be sure, and several strands of dark, coarse hair were stuck to the bumper and front wheel.

The officer scratched his head and phoned in his bizarre report.

For the Fort Lauderdale police department, the night was only beginning.

An hour or so later, the switchboard lit up with calls from other motorists who had apparently encountered either the same "creature" or one just like it. Amid chuckles and hee-haws, a full-scale hunt was launched for what some thought might be an escaped gorilla or other wild animal.

At 2:12 a.m., patrolman Robert Hollemeyal thought he saw something resembling the creature ambling down a highway. The officer got out of his car, drew his revolver, and ordered it to halt—in English, of course.

When the creature screamed at him in a high-pitched, threatening manner, Hollemeyal opened fire with two rounds. The shambling mass of hair and arms screamed again, then jumped twenty feet off the road and scurried away at about twenty miles an hour.

Nothing else was seen of the creature, in spite of an all-night search of the area with cars and helicopters. Whatever it was, it was gone now—vanished, perhaps, into a nearby swamp from which it had probably emerged in the first place.

Although the Fort Lauderdale monster is long gone,

memories of it remain. So do those of other hair-raising encounters with similar critters up and down the Sunshine State, from Miami to Jacksonville.

If not escaped gorillas or wild bears, as some have suggested, then what on earth *are* these nightmarish brutes and where do they come from?

Experts disagree, but some think they are similar to Bigfoot of the Pacific Northwest and Sasquatch of Canada. For years Floridians have referred to them as "skunk apes," apparently in reference to their strong smell and ape-like appearance. They are usually described as large, mean, and hairy, often standing well over eight feet tall and weighing close to eight hundred pounds.

Whatever their nature and origin, skunk apes appear here to stay—at least in the minds of many Floridians who claim to have seen them.

Such was the case with Richard Davis, who lived in an isolated area of Cape Coral in the mid-1970s. For several nights in a row, his Alsatian dog had been doing a lot of barking, apparently reacting to some prowler or unknown presence in the woods outside the house.

On the night of February 2, 1975, the dog—a female—was particularly restless. Thinking perhaps a prowler had wandered onto his property, Richard turned his dog loose. A few minutes later, the animal scooted back to the house and cowered beneath a car inside the garage. She was obviously terrified of something out there in the dark.

Davis did what many concerned property owners would have done under similar circumstances—he grabbed his gun and stormed out into the yard.

That's when he saw it, all nine feet of it, looming like a deformed shadow beneath the yellowish glow of his security light. The thing, covered in grayish-brown hair, stood about fifteen feet away, swaying. Davis took one step more and fired point-blank into the creature's massive chest. It grunted once, then darted off into the woods, obviously unfazed.

Unnerved, but still very much in control of his emotions, Davis moved quickly around his house, checking for signs of the creature. He found tracks, lots of tracks, but the thing that disturbed him most was finding a set of footprints on top of the single air conditioning unit.

A few days later, while discussing his uninvited guest with some neighbors, Smith learned that they, too, had been awakened at night by strange sounds in the yard and a particularly foul-smelling odor. They also said unusual tracklike markings had been found on their air conditioners.

A month later, on March 24, another skunk ape incident was reported in Dade County, Florida. About midnight, Michael Bennett and Lawrence Groom were driving along a back road near Black Point and they saw an enormous manlike creature leaning over a parked automobile.

As soon as Bennett and Groom drew near, a hysterical man jumped out and yelled for help. The moment the creature saw the approaching car, it dashed off into a mangrove swamp and disappeared. Officers from the Dade County Public Safety Department searched the area the next day but found no sign of the monster.

As with similar creatures elsewhere, skunk ape sightings in Florida are made by people of all kinds and ages. On October 11, 1975, a 67-year-old minister named S. L. Whatley, of Fort McCoy, Florida, was cutting wood in the Ocala National Forest. It was about 2 p.m. He was tired, having been swinging the chainsaw all morning.

Suddenly, for no reason at all, Whatley got the creepy sensation that *something* was watching him from the woods. Unseen eyes seemed to follow him everywhere he went. It felt as if he were being observed by some curious animal.

Then his worst nightmare stepped out of the shadows.

"It was this hairy-like ape animal standing there in the palmetto bushes," the minister recalled. "It looked to me to be seven or maybe eight feet tall. It had a dark, chocolate-colored face, a face that was clear of hair, and a flat nose. The arms—I couldn't tell what kind of hands it had—the arms were down into the palmetto bushes."

Whatley bolted for his truck, grabbed an axe and turned around to confront the manlike animal.

It was gone.

Though not nearly as famous as Bigfoot, Sasquatch, or the Himalayan yeti, Florida's skunk ape remains one of the South's most enduring, if not lovable, mysteries.

Encounters with the Unknown

Captain Mantell's Final Flight

Since 1947, more than ten thousand sightings of unidentified flying objects have been reported in several southern states. Hardly a month goes by, it seems, without at least one major report appearing in regional newspapers about a UFO incident or some other strange aerial phenomenon.

Probably the strangest—and certainly the most tragic—case involved a young Air National Guard pilot from Godman Field, Kentucky, named Thomas Mantell. In the annals of UFO lore, the Mantell case stands out as one of the most mysterious.

On the afternoon of January 7, 1948, Captain Mantell, an experienced flyer, climbed aboard his F-51 aircraft to take part in a routine training exercise over Godman Field. The day was gloomy and cold, a bad day for flying, and the aviator looked forward to completing the mission and returning home.

Sometime around 1:45 p.m., a control tower operator spotted a strange flying object heading in Mantell's direction. About an hour later—at 2:48 p.m.—Captain Mantell radioed back that he had made visual contact with the unidentified flying object and was in pursuit.

Two other planes in Mantell's formation also saw the object but pulled back when they realized it was climbing beyond 15,000 feet—the maximum altitude for which the aircraft were equipped. Mantell, however, veered ahead of his wingman and continued the upward climb, even though he knew he was risking his life.

A few minutes later he told the tower he was going to 20,000 feet. He described the object as a "large, glowing sphere...tremendous in size," that always managed to stay several hundred yards ahead of him. Mantell nosed his F-51 upward in a steep climb, trying to maintain visual contact with the rapidly ascending UFO.

At exactly 3:50 p.m., the tower lost both visual and audio contact with the captain. Minutes later, a report came in that Mantell's plane had crashed and burned in a nearby field.

Before going down, Mantell gave a final description of the object he was chasing higher and higher into the clouds. Although no official transcript is available, at least one controller in the tower that afternoon swore that Mantell was convinced he was chasing an unknown type of aircraft—perhaps either Russian or Chinese—but certainly not American.

The controller thought Mantell had called it a "flying saucer."

The term "flying saucer" itself had only come into use a few months earlier when an Idaho commercial pilot had so described such an object to reporters. The first known use of the appellation "saucer," however, goes back to 1878 when a farmer used it to describe the shape of an object which he reported over his farm near Denison, Texas.

Until it closed its official study on the subject in 1969, the Air Force and other governmental agencies referred to these strange aerial objects as "U-FOBs," for "unidentified flying objects." Most experts in the field prefer the usage "UFO" rather than flying saucer or disc, since aerial phenomena come in a bewildering variety of shapes and sizes.

It is unlikely that Captain Mantell, on that fateful day forty-one years ago, had ever even heard of UFOs.

What happened isn't clear. Some investigators think Mantell probably blacked out from lack of oxygen and his plane simply crashed to the earth. Others aren't so sure, however. One retired Air Force officer who helped investigate the crash said Mantell—an experienced pilot all too aware of the dangers of anoxia (oxygen starvation) above 15,000 feet—

was drawn into the clouds against his will.

As for Mantell's "large, glowing object," it was probably nothing more than Venus rising or an enormous skyhook balloon—or so said military officials at the scene of the crash. Coral E. Lorenzen, author of *Flying Saucers: the Startling Evidence of the Invasion From Outer Space* and a long-time researcher in the field of aerial phenomena, thinks otherwise.

"I am not prepared to dispute this theory," wrote Lorenzen, "except to say that no balloon flight for that particular area has been discovered in military archives....As far as I'm concerned, the Mantell case should be listed as 'unknown' until the 'object' can be positively identified."

As for the Venus theory, Lorenzen says the fallacy of that explanation was evident. "Venus was not at maximum magnitude at that specific time, and although Venus can be seen on clear days at peak brilliance—if one knows where to look—it would have been impossible for Mantell to chase something that would not have been visible on that partly cloudy day."

But the biggest surprise was yet to come.

When Mantell's plane went down, slamming into the earth at hundreds of miles an hour, investigators quickly swarmed onto the crash site, sifting, poking, and probing through the charred wreckage. Suddenly someone realized that the pilot's body was missing! It was as if Mantell had simply disappeared from the cockpit.

According to Lorenzen, Mantell's body was never found. Its whereabouts, says the writer who spent years researching the Mantell case, remains one of the greatest mysteries in UFO lore.

One leading expert, a retired captain in the reserves who took part in the investigation, believes the pilot was removed alive from the crippled aircraft by the very spaceship he was chasing.

Arkansas's Strange Voyager from the Stars

Since earliest times men have looked toward the sky for answers to many of life's most compelling questions: Who are we? Where did we come from? Where are we going?

Thousands of years ago, civilizations in the Middle East turned to the heavens for clues to universal purpose. Complex sky-charts were developed not only to help keep track of celestial movements but also to interpret natural phenomena. Thunder, lightning, and other strange atmospheric disturbances were constant reminders that man was not alone, that supernatural forces far beyond the stars controlled our earth-bound spirits and influenced our own development.

It was only natural, then, that concepts of God and Heaven would become associated with the sky. The sky was seen as a veiled, mystical doorway to Heaven—a vast, wondrous dome, sometimes pleasant, sometimes moody, but always full of mystery.

Whenever a thunderstorm struck, it was invariably linked to some higher power. Whenever ball lightning flared in the middle of a swamp, or a shower of meteors blazed across a velvet sky, the temptation was always strong to regard it as divine intervention.

Along with divine inspiration and wonder, the sky also brought terror. The Bible and other ancient manuscripts are full of unearthly events emanating from the heavens— flaming balls of fire, burning chariots, titanic winds, and the like. Even today, as spaceships orbit the planets and plunge far out into space, whenever something bad goes wrong down here on earth, our first reaction is to lift our thoughts toward Heaven.

Such was the case on the afternoon of December 8, 1847, in the tiny Arkansas town of Forest Hill.

The day had dawned clear and cold, but sometime after lunch, a few gray clouds started blowing in from the east. Shoppers, bundled against the blustery winter chill, scurried along the sidewalks, taking advantage of pre-Christmas sales. The smell of burning wood, mixed with the aroma of baked goods, lay heavy over the town square.

Later in the day, the clouds grew dark and angry.

One observer described them as a "solid black fleece lighted from above by a red glare as of many torches."

It was an eerie phenomenon, certainly unlike anything the people of Forest Hill had ever seen. Curious shopkeepers and customers rushed into the streets to watch what appeared to be a gathering storm. Powerful winds gusted down Main Street, rattling glass windows and overturning public benches. Bonnets and hats flew in every direction, as crowds of people staggered and stumbled along the dusty sidewalks and streets.

Lightning flashed and popped. Thunder roared and grumbled. At three o'clock a freezing rain started to fall in sheets. Pedestrians scampered for cover. They huddled inside shops and houses and beneath rickety storefront overhangs, waiting for the storm to pass.

Suddenly a loud explosion split the dark skies. After the explosion came a rumble—a rumble so long and deep it caused houses to wobble and rattled the church bell.

A few seconds later a "barrel-sized flaming body" crashed into the earth just outside the town, kicking up a cloud of smoke and steam half a mile high. When a handful of brave citizens went to investigate, they found a gaping hole in the ground. The hole measured eight feet deep and two feet in diameter.

At the bottom of the hole, still smoldering, was a large,

odd-shaped rock. The smell of sulphur lay heavy over the site. When someone threw a bucket of water onto the rock, the hole hissed and spewed steam, reminding those present of an erupting volcano.

What was it?

No one had the slightest clue.

One man fell to his knees and began to pray. Another started to climb down inside the hole but a tangle of brawny arms pulled him back. Better to leave it alone, they felt, at least until the thing could be properly identified.

Twenty minutes later, the rain stopped and the sun peeked out from behind a gently fading cloud. The storm had passed. Relieved faces peered toward a dazzling, freshly-scrubbed sky.

Although the object that crashed into the ground just outside Forest Hill has long since disappeared, scientists still wonder about its origins. Was it a meteorite, as some suspect, or was it something else—perhaps an abnormal byproduct of lighting called a fulgurite?

Those who say it was a meteorite, however, cannot account for the violent, bewildering storm that preceded the object's fall to earth. Meteors generally pass through earth's atmosphere quickly, sometimes taking only a few seconds before impacting with earth. And since meteors have no control over weather, its crash during the storm would have been nothing more than coincidental.

A commonly held theory about the Forest Hill strike is that a bolt of lightning, the likes of which had never been seen in Arkansas, sliced into the earth, fusing the sand into a solid mass at the bottom of the hole. Such a mass, known as fulgurite, is not uncommon.

Few scientists believe that's what happened, however.

The enormous size of the rocky object itself has led many experts to conclude it would have been impossible for a single bolt of lightning to have caused such a large fulgurite.

While the experts argued, a few residents of the tiny town had their own ideas about what happened. Clearly, said some, it was a message from God, a sign that something was wrong spiritually with their community. In the following weeks, faithful flocks gathered behind church doors and beneath revival tents to pray and debate about the mysterious voyager from the stars.

The Patriot's *Last Voyage*

One cold winter morning in 1813, residents of Nags Head, a tiny coastal community in North Carolina, awoke to an astonishing sight. Down on the beach, bobbing in the frothy surf, was a large, handsomely appointed schooner which had apparently washed ashore during the night.

When investigators reached the ship, they made a startling discovery—there was nobody on board! Except for a scrawny black kitten found in the kitchen, the ship was completely deserted. Apparently the vessel had been abandoned offshore, but that didn't seem to make sense because no lifeboats were missing. Also, except for some minor damage to the keel, the ship appeared to be in excellent condition.

According to one witness, "all the sails were still set on the vessel, the rudder was lashed, and the craft seemed to be in good order, but entirely deserted." In one of the cabins were fancy silk dresses, a vase of beautiful flowers, and the portrait of a lovely young woman in white.

Determined to get to the bottom of the mystery, investigators continued a cabin-to-cabin search for clues. They found nothing—no note, log or record that might explain the identity of the lonely schooner or the whereabouts of its missing passengers and crew. It was as if everyone on board the ship had simply disappeared—vanished into the unknown without a trace.

A few weeks earlier, a New York-bound schooner named the *Patriot* had disappeared shortly after sailing from

Georgetown, South Carolina. No trace of the *Patriot,* a former New York pilot boat and privateer, had been found, in spite of one of the largest search and rescue operations in American history at the time. Could the schooner that drifted ashore at Nags Head be the *Patriot?*

Incredibly, no officials from New York came down to North Carolina to investigate, and with the war with England going on, fearful Carolinians had other things on their minds besides trying to determine the identity of a shipwreck. The mysterious schooner on the beach was soon forgotten.

But public interest in the fate of the *Patriot* never went away. More than one hundred seventy years later, the strange disappearance of the men, women, and children aboard the vessel remains one of maritime history's greatest unsolved mysteries. Many theories have come and gone, but so far no one has been able to answer the crucial question—what happened to the passengers and crew?

Perhaps the incident wouldn't have aroused such intense national and international interest had it not been for the fact that one of the passengers—Theodosia Burr Alston—was the wife of John Alston, governor of South Carolina, and the daughter of Aaron Burr, controversial former vice-president of the United States.

Frail, sickly, and depressed over the recent loss of her only child, Theodosia was on her way to visit relatives in New York when the *Patriot* disappeared shortly after setting sail from Georgetown, South Carolina, on December 30, 1812. Theodosia, twenty-nine years old and already one of the most gifted gentlewomen of her day, had other reasons to be depressed. Only recently her father had shot and killed Alexander Hamilton during a duel. Acquitted of that charge, he was now being tried for treason in an alleged scheme to set up a new government in Texas and Mexico.

When the *Patriot* failed to arrive on schedule in New York, an intensive search and rescue operation was launched. Investigators manning private and federally-registered vessels combed the entire eastern seaboard for signs of the missing vessel, even checking ports as far south as Nassau. For some inexplicable reason, they never bothered to follow up on the report that an unidentified schooner had washed up on the storm-scarred beach at Nags Head.

Six months earlier, the United States had declared war on Great Britain. It was a known fact that British warships prowled American waters, but the London government emphatically denied any involvement with the *Patriot* affair. There were other possibilities. Privateers and pirates also roamed the eastern sea lanes, preying on small civilian vessels like the *Patriot*. As improbable as it sounded, the *Patriot* might have fallen victim to a pirate ship.

Two decades later, in 1833, an article in an Alabama newspaper reawakened interest in the *Patriot*. A man who resided "in one of the interior counties of this state" reportedly made a deathbed confession linking him and several other companions to the capture of the *Patriot*. In an article published in the Mobile *Press-Register,* the unidentified man swore he had participated in the murder of "of all those on board," and the scuttling of the vessel "for the sake of her plate and effects."

Fifteen years later another confessed pirate told a similar deathbed story, adding that one of the passengers on board the captured vessel was a woman named "Odessa Burr Alston," who had, when given the alternative of sharing a cabin with the pirate captain, chosen death.

In the following years, numerous other stories surfaced about the fate of the *Patriot,* some of them quite fanciful. One version held that a sea monster crawled aboard and devoured everyone, then slithered back into the sea. Another held that the entire crew and passengers were being held hostage on a tiny island in the Bahamas.

It now seems probable that the schooner that drifted ashore at Nags Head in January 1813 was, indeed, the *Patriot*. The key clue was the portrait of a young woman found in one of the cabins, identified years later by family members as Theodosia Burr Alston. Still, the fate of Theodosia and the other passengers and crew of the *Patriot* remains one of North Carolina's greatest maritime mysteries.

Invisible Residents of the Deep

On July 5, 1965, an unusual story appeared on the wires of the Associated Press.

While conducting one-man submarine operations off the coast of Pierce, Florida, an oceanographer named Dmitri Rebikoff was startled when an unusually long, pear-shaped object shot up from the clear, blue depths toward him.

At first he thought it was a shark, which seemed reasonable enough. That area of the ocean was known to be teeming with the creatures.

But there was something *unusual* about the form slicing quickly through the waters, something that didn't seem quite right. As Rebikoff later told Captain L. Jacques Nicholas, coordinator of the undersea project, the thing coming toward him seemed off and unnatural, very much out of place in the water.

It definitely wasn't a shark.

"Its direction and speed were too constant," the scientist explained in the AP interview. "It may have been running on a robot pilot. We received no signal (from it) and therefore do not know what it was."

Rebikoff reportedly took photographs, but according to the AP report, "(t)he film was not processed immediately" and somehow got misplaced.

What sounds like just another case of underwater heebie-jeebies could be more—much more, if you ask Ivan T. Sanderson, a world-famous naturalist and author who has investigated hundreds of similar incidents over the years.

Sanderson's conclusion is that the object spotted by Dmitri could have been a UAO—or unidentified aerial object, as he prefers to call the phenomena more conventionally known as UFOs, unidentified flying objects.

If anyone knows about such things, it should be Sanderson.

For years, the distinguished student of the paranormal has roamed the world accumulating data and interviewing people who have experienced similar phenomena. In his bestselling book *Invisible Residents,* the scientist lays out his now-famous notion that unidentified beings—possibly from outer space—have been living in the oceans, lakes, and deeper rivers of the world for centuries, conducting covert operations for reasons known only to them.

It's Sanderson's opinion that the secretive activity beneath the still waters of the world should be studied more closely—for national security if for no other reason.

"When it comes to something like underwater UAOs, we find that *nobody* really has a clue as to what is going on. Let us not forget that the poor so-called armed services—the armies, navies, and air forces—are only 'junior' executives with very specific terms of reference. They are not scientists or even technologists...." Yet "the poor fellows" have the responsibility of solving some of the world's greatest unsolved mysteries—UAOs.

Before we rush to banish Dr. Sanderson and his ideas to the realm of La-la-land, let us hear him out. The man is as well known and respected as he is controversial and daring. His many books on nature and natural phenomena, including *Animal Treasure, Living Treasure,* and *Uninvited Visitors,* have been hailed by the academic community as well as general public.

When Ivan T. Sanderson bothers to write a book on a particular subject, regardless of how bizarre, it will be not only well-written and fun to read, but also thoroughly researched and documented, supported usually by charts, appendices, references, and ample footnotes to guide the scholar as well as casual reader.

That said, let us now get back to the task at hand—hearing what Sanderson has to say about UAOs and their link to the strange things reportedly going on below the surface of our globe's oceans, lakes, and rivers.

It is Sanderson's suspicion that historical and recent sightings of lighted objects rising from, hovering over, or descending into oceans and lakes around the world *are* all indeed somehow linked. He correlates such superficially unrelated studies as analyses by engineers of ancient art objects that may represent air-to-water craft, the appearance of wheels of light, the time-speed incongruities experienced by flyers, and the disappearance without a trace of air and water craft and of shipboard travelers in certain "lozenge-shaped" areas around the world.

"These matters," he says, "would seem to have nothing more in common than that they all have something to do with water. There is, nonetheless, an underlying unity...as possible aspects of and evidence for an overall concept...that there is an underwater civilization (or civilizations) on this planet that has been here for a very long time and which has evolved here, and/or that there are intelligent entities who have been coming here from elsewhere...which prefer to use the bottom of the hydrosphere...in which to reside and from which to operate."

Since about seventy-five percent of the earth's surface is covered with water, it seems logical that such "civilizations" could flourish, unseen and undetected even by modern submarines and sonar devices.

More than fifty percent of all sightings of so-called UAOs "have occurred over, coming from, going away over, or plunging into or coming out of water." Sanderson believes that's proof enough that science should be focusing its resources and energies on understanding what's going on *under* the sea rather than above it in the air.

"Does this not have any significance?" he asks. "Nearly three-quarters of the surface of our planet is covered with water; but, despite airplanes now flying over the oceans, and boating going on all about, we have only a minute portion of this vast aqueous area under regular surveillance.

"Have we been ignoring the mountain of evidence that something is happening down there?"

For years that "mountain of evidence" has been slowly building. In late 1954, for example, the Navy Hydrographic Office reported that an American fuel tanker, *Dynafuel,* watched an eerie cloud of smoke rising from the waters of the Gulf of Mexico.

Upon closer examination, "the smoke appeared to come from *under water* and resembled smoke from bombs dropped during target practice," the ship's master said. "It lasted only ten minutes."

There was no official explanation, even though the NHO conducted a thorough search of the area for downed aircraft or missing ships.

In July of 1961, a 67-foot shrimp boat owned by Ira Pete was cruising off Port Aransas in the Gulf of Mexico when she "hooked into something that ripped the vessel's stern right off." Although Pete and his two crewmen survived, they were unable to say what that "something" was.

Five years later, in 1966, two divers from the Naval Ordinance Laboratory Test Facility accompanied Martin Meylach, an amateur treasure hunter, on a dive just off the coast of Miami, Florida. The men were working in about forty feet of crystal-clear water when they discovered a long cylindrical object that resembled a rocket.

The incident was reported to naval officials at Homestead Air Force Base, who quickly moved in to investigate. A spokesman said he had no idea where the strange mechanism had come from and discounted theories that it was some sort of missile dropped by craft from a nearby base.

Although Sanderson agrees with mainstream science that most sightings of UAOs or UFOs can be easily attributed to meteorological phenomena, weather balloons, and other rational explanations, he thinks that a surprisingly large number cannot and therefore remain essentially unsolved. What concerns him, however, is not the number of unsolved UAO cases but the way the general public and popular media sensationalize such sightings, especially those observed by trained professional people.

"Despite what anybody may have told you—be they the working press, the 'experts,' the run-of-the-mill scientists and technologists, or even officialdom—don't be put off or misled," he urges. "Read for yourself what hard facts there are on record, and then draw your own conclusions."

*Lost Causes and
Blood-stained Myths*

The Gray Ghost of the Confederacy

Near the end of the Civil War, gangs of "border outlaws" roamed the rugged backcountry of the divided nation's heartland, robbing, burning, and killing anybody who got in their way. Although some of them fought in the name of the Confederacy, most were simply in it for the money.

One such man was William Clarke Quantrill, alias "The Gray Ghost." Elusive, shadowy, always on the run, Quantrill and his band of rowdy rebels blazed a bloody trail of terror from Texas to Kentucky before a Union patrol finally caught up with him one morning in the waning days of the war.

Before he died in a hail of bullets, Quantrill reportedly told his men to "keep up the fight....Don't allow the Confederacy to fall...."

Rumors persisted that he somehow survived the fierce battle and actually plotted to restore the fallen Confederacy years later. Legends about the Gray Ghost's unwavering loyalty to the Stars and Bars, his uncertain fate, and his mysterious plans to help the South rise again continue to intrigue historians more than one hundred twenty-five years after Appomattox.

According to some sources, Quantrill—who was on his way to Washington to assassinate Abraham Lincoln—was killed when his unit accidentally encountered a group of Union soldiers at Wakefield Farm in Kentucky. Other accounts say he was captured and executed afterwards.

Yet another story, still much debated, suggests that Quantrill escaped from the ambush and didn't actually die until after the turn of the century. That story is usually linked with other legends about Quantrill's missing treasure and secret plans to restore the old Confederacy.

During his days as a guerrilla leader, Quantrill reportedly stole millions in gold, silver, and cash from Northern banks and Union Army payloads. The loot, buried at several locations throughout the South, was going to be used to finance the new uprising—or so the legend goes.

Unfortunately, other leading members of Quantrill's inner circle either died or disappeared, and no trace of the treasure was ever found. Quantrill himself was never seen or heard from again, although rumors continued to crop up in the early 1900s that he was holed up at several locations in the South.

Ironically, the man who gave the Union Army and Northern sympathizers so much trouble had been born a Yankee himself. The son of an Ohio schoolteacher, Quantrill also taught school for a while, then headed west with his brother in a covered wagon.

Fate overtook the young brothers in Kansas. One night a group of about thirty "Red Legs" rode into camp, killing Quantrill's brother and leaving him for dead. When he came to three days later, wounded and bleeding, he swore revenge on the gang. With the aid of an old Indian, Quantrill was able to track down and kill all but three of the murderers.

When the war broke out, Quantrill found himself leaning toward the Confederate cause. Some biographers say his decision was linked to the death of his brother at the hands of the northern agitators. But James M. McPherson, author of the bestselling *Battle Cry of Freedom,* suggests Quantrill chose the Confederate ideology "apparently because...this allowed him to attack all symbols of authority."

And attack he did. Moving quickly, Quantrill—Captain Quantrill, now—formed a band of rowdy followers who shared both his burning hatred for Yankees and desire to line his pockets with easy money. "Quantrill's Raiders," as the gang came to be known, eventually attracted such infamous desperados as Frank and Jesse James, the Dalton brothers, and the Younger brothers.

One of Quantrill's lieutenants was William "Bloody Bill" Anderson, perhaps the most ruthless slayer of innocent people in American history. Anderson's band showed no mercy. Striking at isolated garrisons and small posts, he and his cohorts murdered thousands of men, women and children—including unarmed soldiers—and sometimes scalped their victims.

In most parts of the South, however, Quantrill was seen as a hero, a gallant Confederate crusader fighting for the cause. With cape flying and sword flashing, Quantrill proved to be a formidable foe even against superior forces. General Sterling Price was so impressed by Quantrill's prowess that he openly praised the commander for the "gallant struggle you have made against despotism and the oppression of our State (Missouri)."

North of the Mason-Dixon line, the Gray Ghost was regarded as a common thug, a "border ruffian" who mutilated innocent people for pleasure, put towns to the torch, and garrotted unarmed soldiers—all in the name of the Confederacy.

Throughout the country, Quantrill's reputation as a fierce warrior continued to grow, along with his seemingly undisciplined enthusiasm to commit dastardly deeds. After a group of rebel wives were killed by Union soldiers in Lawrence, Kansas, Quantrill's men thundered into town with orders to "kill every male and burn every house."

The battle raged for more than three hours. When the smoke had cleared, one hundred eighty-two men and boys lay dead in the blood-stained streets of Lawrence, and one hundred eighty-five buildings had burned to the ground.

Over the years, many legends about this enigmatic, almost mythological rebel chieftain continued to grow. It is still difficult to distinguish fact from folklore. Some put his place of birth in Maryland, others Pennsylvania. One source claims he was a deeply religious man, a former schoolteacher intent on seeking his fortune out west when the war broke out and changed his life forever.

Not a few of Quantrill's critics, however, assert he was nothing but a no-account drifter with bloodthirsty habits. They say he used the Civil War as an excuse to prey upon innocent victims and didn't mind slaughtering anybody who got in his way.

Quantrill's relationship with famous outlaws and gunslingers also remains steeped in mystery and legend. There seems strong evidence that he not only knew the Dalton Gang, the Younger brothers, and Frank and Jesse James, but that they also worked for him during the war.

In his memoirs, Captain Kit Dalton, who went on to achieve his own black fame as a guerrilla outlaw long after the war had ended, defended Quantrill as a "man of dignity and the highest calling."

"The idea seems...in many sections that Quantrill...was an outlaw whose sole object in life was to prey indiscriminately...and to kill all who opposed his undertakings," Dalton wrote. "Nothing could be more ridiculous. Quantrill was never an outlaw, but a soldier whose genius and energy in behalf of the Southern people made the world ring with his daring exploits."

While some historians disagree over Quantrill's personal motives, all generally agree on his tactics. According to McPherson, Quantrill attracted to his gang "some of the most psychopathic killers in American history. In kaleidoscopic fashion, groups of these men would split off to form their own bands and then come together again for larger raids.

Although the motives of these men centered on robbery, revenge and a "nihilistic love of violence," McPherson contends they were also influenced by ideology.

"They fought for slavery and Confederate independence."

The Cruel Mistress of Royal Street

Back in the days before the Civil War, Delphine McCarty was one of the most beautiful and popular young ladies in New Orleans. Sweet, charming, always polite and gushing with affection, this dark-eyed French-Irish belle captured the hearts of more than her fair share of handsome young men of social standing.

When she finally married a wealthy New Orleans banker just after the turn of the century, it was said that a number of broken-hearted suitors left town. One who remained, however, was a rising young legislator who would get a second chance to propose when Delphine's first husband died shortly after their honeymoon.

The grief-stricken widow wasted no time accepting the legislator's proposal. Less than six months later they were married. At first, everything seemed to be going fine with the new marriage. There were countless balls and outings in the country, even a couple of trips to Europe. As one acquaintance of the couple put it: "The marriage was made in Heaven."

But heaven turned into hell a short time later when Delphine's second husband also died. The circumstances surrounding the young legislator's death were never fully revealed, but rumor had it he was murdered—poisoned, to be precise.

Predictably, the French Quarter was soon abuzz with gossip. In private drawing rooms and in the moss-draped shadows of cobblestoned courtyards, it was being whispered that Delphine herself was the murderer—that she had killed her first two husbands for insurance money. No charges were brought, and in time the rumors went away.

Then, in 1825, Delphine met a prominent middle-aged physician named Louis Lalaurie. It was love at first sight for the twice-widowed woman, now forty-five. A few months later wedding bells chimed once more in her honor.

Delphine's marriage to Dr. Lalaurie was one of the most talked about social events of the decade. Hundreds of guests were invited to the ceremony and reception, including most of New Orleans' leading citizens. The happy couple bought a handsome new house at the corner of Royal and Governor Nichols streets, where for years they continued to entertain in lavish style. Senators, congressmen, bankers, lawyers, and a number of national and international celebrities— including the Marquis de Lafayette himself—were frequent visitors to the sprawling, three-story residence at 1140 Royal Street.

The Lalaurie house was one of the finest and largest in all of New Orleans. Built during the time of Napoleon in French Empire style, it was highlighted by elegant iron grillwork, black-and-white marble flooring, large, richly-ornamented drawing rooms, and one of the most handsome mahogany-railed staircases in the South.

Especially noteworthy was its striking roof-top cupola, from which visitors could look out over the Mississippi River on one side and Congo Square on the other. It was said that Madame Lalaurie grew particularly fond of hiking up to the cupola late at night, where she would spend hours watching the Negroes dance wildly to the beat of voodoo drums down on the square.

Soon after settling in her new house, Madame Lalaurie became the target of more strange rumors swirling through the neighborhood. People who put two and two together began to suspect her of mistreating her slaves. Some said she flogged them. It was true that many of her black domestics appeared weak and listless whenever company came around, and that many disappeared without ever being accounted for.

There was even a story that Madame Lalaurie kept her black cook chained to the fireplace!

Some close neighbors reported hearing screams in the middle of the night—screams that seemed to come from the basement of the Lalaurie house. The final proof that something was out of the ordinary occurred one day when a passerby happened to observe Madame Lalaurie chasing a young black girl with a stick. While the passerby watched, Madame Lalaurie reportedly chased the girl up a back stairway leading toward the rooftop, screaming at the top of her lungs.

When the little girl reached the top and had nowhere else to run, she jumped off the house rather than be caught by the pursuing white woman. She was killed instantly, her small, frail body dashed against the cobblestone driveway below.

During the investigation, authorities ordered the entire house searched. This was against Madame Lalaurie's wishes, but she was pushed aside as policemen broke through a door leading down into the basement. There, in the musty bowels of the Lalaurie mansion, the officers made a grisly discovery. A group of nine slaves lay chained to the floor, their naked, emaciated bodies barely able to move. Bones poked through the thin flesh of their arms, legs, and faces, and most of them wore iron-spiked collars that kept their heads in one position.

Nearby stood a low platform and a cowhide whip stiff with blood. In the course of the investigation, it was learned that every morning for the past several years, Madame Lalaurie had gone down into the crypt, climbed up on the platform, and whipped the slaves senseless with the burr-tipped cowhide.

While the policemen were distracted, Madame Lalaurie climbed into her coach and escaped. Crowds of angry citizens reportedly chased her as far as Lake Pontchartrain, but lost her when she hopped aboard a ferryboat. She was never seen again, although it was often reported that the once-popular belle of New Orleans had become a court favorite in Paris.

For years, many of Madame Lalaurie's devoted friends refused to believe she could have been responsible for so much cruelty. "How could she?" one gentleman friend asked. "She was a kind, caring person—quite incapable of harming a fly."

The mystery of Madame Lalaurie's dark side was one thing, but the controversial stories that soon emerged about her abandoned old residence were quite another.

It seems the Lalaurie house was haunted—haunted by the ghosts of Madame's victims and the dark demons that possessed her soul. The house itself soon fell into ruin, but not before a lot of strange tales began surfacing about eerie lights glowing in windows late at night, sinister shadows flickering across the moss-hung courtyard, and skeletal hands appearing at the front door.

There were sounds, too—blood-curdling shrieks and moans and a woman's high-pitched laughter as leather lashed against shredded flesh. One of the most frequently reported sounds was that of a jangling chain being dragged down an empty staircase inside the house.

Even in recent times, credible witnesses have seen the ghostly form of a little black girl floating across the courtyard. Some claim to seen the ghost leap from the top of the house in a macabre re-enactment of the death scene.

Today the Lalaurie mansion is a private residence, but it remains one of New Orleans' most famous haunted houses.

Did Davy Crockett
Really Die at the Alamo?

On March 29, 1836, a curious article appeared on the front page of the *Arkansas Gazette*. A staff-written story quoted two unidentified men—both badly wounded—who claimed they had survived the bloody massacre at the Alamo a few days earlier.

In fact, said the two, several other Texans had walked away from the tiny garrison as well—including perhaps the most famous Indian-fighter of all time, Davy Crockett himself.

But wait—something seems to be wrong here.

Don't our history books tell us that Crockett died "fighting like a tiger" atop the ramparts of the Alamo as thousands of Santa Anna's troops swarmed over the tiny garrison? Haven't books been written and movies made showing how Crockett, Jim Bowie, Col. William Travis, and about one hundred eighty-one other brave Texans fought to the bitter end against overwhelming military odds?

Today, more than a century and a half after the fall of the Alamo, historians are taking another look at the famous battle and the shroud of myths that has enveloped it ever since. Some of the facts emerging appear to contradict several time-honored claims about that struggle and the gallant band of heroes who squared off against Santa Anna's "invincible" army.

There is evidence, for example, that suggests Travis, the

commander of the garrison, was not killed by enemy troops, but instead committed suicide. And while Bowie—knife fighter, Louisiana slave smuggler, land speculator, and seller of fraudulent land claims—did in fact die in bed as commonly believed, some of his buckskinned compatriots actually threw down their weapons and surrendered.

Most startling of all is the possibility that Davy Crockett, "king of the wild frontier" and one of America's most beloved heroes, was among those who surrendered. Based on eyewitness accounts, diaries, and sworn statements from Mexican officers at the scene, Crockett is believed by some to have been among eight Texans who were executed shortly after the hostilities by Santa Anna.

If this "new" information is correct, then why has it taken so long for the record to be set straight? Why have historians led us down the yellow brick road toward myth and legend for so long?

The answer to these questions probably has more to do with the intense spirit of nationalism sweeping the country in the early days of the 19th century than anything else. American settlers in Mexican territory, caught up in the beguiling spell of Manifest Destiny, were agitating strongly for statehood by the early 1830s. This, of course, was frowned upon by the Mexican government, especially after Antonio Lopez de Santa Anna came to power in 1833.

When the new generalissimo overthrew the old Mexican constitution, proclaimed himself supreme dictator, and began pressing Texans for additional taxes, the Americans reacted by seizing two small garrisons—one at Anahuac and the other at San Antonio. Santa Anna, who compared himself with Napoleon, responded to the insurrection by leading an army northward across the Rio Grande.

In February 1836, several thousand crack Mexican troops reached San Antonio and surrounded the tiny Alamo.

When Travis, a tall, blue-eyed lawyer from Alabama refused to surrender, Santa Anna lay siege. Finally, thirteen days later, the Mexican army launched an all-out assault on the old Spanish mission that had hastily been converted into a fort by the Texans.

Under a "great round southern moon" they came, eight thousand or more, drums beating, banners flying, sabers gleaming. While artillery roared in the distance, wave after wave of cavalrymen charged, followed by swarms of infantrymen. The fighting was fierce but brief.

When the smoke had cleared, all one hundred eighty-four defenders were dead. According to most accounts of the episode, a few women and children were allowed to go free, along with an old black slave named Joe. Because of their dramatic stand, the men of the Alamo were seen as martyrs and made legend. Their story became one of the most celebrated in American history; then and thereafter, the Alamo stood as a symbol of duty and heroic sacrifice against overwhelming odds.

Today, far removed from the impassioned atmosphere that prevailed following the slaughter, some scholars are openly criticizing the traditional account of what happened at the Alamo. In fact, says historian Walter Lord, author of *A Time to Stand*—the most accurate and illuminating book yet written about the Alamo—the historical record has been grossly distorted.

"Folklore has always flowed through the saga of the Alamo, and it is not at all likely to stop," he said.

Lord maintains, for example, that the notion that all the defenders were wiped out has been shown to be untrue. The men interviewed in the *Arkansas Gazette* are just two of several known survivors. Others include a "tough little ex-jockey" from Arkansas and a Mexican national named Brigido Guerrero, who "talked himself free by claiming to have been a prisoner of the Texans."

Even more amazing is the revelation about Crockett's surrender. Lord said news of the famed "Coonskin Congressman" from Tennessee's fate, along with that of the seven other condemned Texans, first surfaced when the schooner *Comanche* reached New Orleans with word of the massacre. Another version of the story appeared in a July edition of the Detroit *Democratic Free Press,* as related by a young Michigan volunteer named George Dolson.

Another myth that sprang up shortly after the massacre concerned the size of Santa Anna's army. Exaggerated accounts say more than eight thousand experienced Mexican troops attacked the Alamo. Actually, says Lord, only six hundred took part initially, while a total of eighteen hundred stormed the mission's walls.

"Many of these were bedraggled Mayan conscripts, who did not even understand the language," Lord wrote. "Their smooth-bore muskets were completely outclassed—the range was only 70 yards—and most of the men didn't know how to aim them."

On the other hand, the Texans defending the Alamo were excellent marksmen and had in their possession twenty-one cannons—"perhaps the largest collection between New Orleans and Mexico City."

New research critical of commonly held beliefs about the Alamo and the brave men who fought and died there does not detract from the historic feat itself. According to Lord, it merely helps explain away some of the myths about our mysterious and sometimes troubling past.

Yet the myth of the Alamo and its glorious stand lives on, ingrained in our collective national consciousness. Like all such events—Bunker Hill, Gettysburg, and Custer's Last Stand—the Alamo, too, has its legends.

The Day Death Came to the Everglades

Into the gloomy wilds of Florida's Everglades there once came a stranger whose dark and bloody deeds would forever haunt that time-forgotten region.

The man's name was Edgar Watson, but nobody ever learned where he came from or what had brought him to the swamp in the first place. Rumor had it he was a Scotsman, probably because of his long red hair, pasty skin, and burning blue eyes.

The mysterious newcomer built himself a small cabin above an old sand-and-shell Indian mound where he had a commanding view of the swirling Chatham River. He planted a garden amid the palms and mangroves and flaming poinciana trees. He grew sugar cane and trapped alligators for a living.

By day, Watson liked to fish and hunt among the silent glades and quivering bogs surrounding his rustic homestead. At night, he'd sit on his front porch overlooking the river, listening to the bullfrogs and counting the stars.

For the most part, Watson kept to himself. Whenever he went into town—which usually meant either Fort Myers or the tiny hamlet of Chokoloskee—he avoided people. As one local put it, "He'd say hello, and that was about it."

Aside from his peculiar aversion to people, there was something else about the stranger that bothered a lot of his neighbors. Although he was generally polite and cordial in the company of others, the red-haired Scotsman always seemed nervous and never turned his back on anybody. That seemed strange to some folks, but not much was made of it at the time.

Eventually word got around that Watson had once killed a man. Later that story was modified to include several victims. One story had it that the fierce-looking newcomer had even gunned down Belle Starr, the notorious lady outlaw of Wild West fame.

Until one day in 1910, there wasn't a shred of evidence to back up any of those claims.

It was then that an unidentified fisherman and his son paddling up the Chatham River near Watson's place happened to notice something odd floating in the black water. Upon closer observation they realized to their horror it was the body of an old woman—carved and gutted, but not bad enough to make it sink.

Their first impulse was to report the find to Watson, thinking perhaps he could identify the unfortunate corpse. At the last minute, however, they changed their minds and decided to drag the grisly find into town and show the sheriff.

On the way, they stopped off at a local country store. A young black boy standing at the back of the store piped up when he heard them telling a group of locals about the corpse in the river. "That ain't nothing," the boy said, shrugging. "That old place up there is crawling with bodies. There's dead people buried everywhere in them woods of Mr. Watson's."

The boy then explained that he had once worked for Watson. On several occasions he had watched his boss kill people, then either bury them in the woods or dump them in the river. Usually he'd disembowel his victims first, so they'd sink to the bottom rather than float. The boy explained that he had escaped with his life by running away.

Then someone in the crowd remembered that a lot of people had been seen heading out to Watson's place over the years—outsiders mostly, men, women, even some children.

Nobody had thought much about it at the time, just that they were migrant workers who would put in a season for Watson, then move on. Funny thing, though—none of the workers was ever seen leaving Watson's place!

Alarmed by the boy's report, a group of townsmen went to the sheriff and reiterated the story. After one look at the corpse, the sheriff quickly organized a posse, gave them guns, and set off for Watson's place.

It didn't take them long to confirm the boy's story. Just about everywhere they dug, human bones turned up—arms, legs, skulls, whole skeletons. There was never any official count, but one source put the number of bodies at two dozen—all in varying states of decomposition.

The river yielded even more corpses—men, women, and children, all ages and colors. Many of the victims had obviously been dead a long time. The sheriff theorized what some of the other men had suspected all along—the dead were all hired hands and their families. The red-haired Scotsman had apparently shot them all to avoid having to pay their salaries.

There was no sign on the place of either Watson or his overseer, a man named Cox. Watson, however, showed up the next day, apparently returning from a fishing trip up the river. When he stopped off at a nearby store, word spread, and soon the sheriff and a posse came running.

Seeing that he was armed, the sheriff walked slowly up to the suspect and said: "Give me your gun, Watson." Watson was quick to realize what was coming down. Instead of doing as the sheriff ordered, he reportedly snapped, "I give my gun to no man," then yanked out his revolver and shot the sheriff square in the chest.

The lawman fell to the floor. Before Watson could draw aim again, however, every man in the posse cut loose with their shotguns and rifles. Years later, men in that part of the swamp still argued over whose bullet had been the one that penetrated Watson's heart. Because so many bullets and buckshot had riddled his body, no one could ever know for sure.

Edgar "Bloody" Watson's body was dragged downriver

to an oyster bank where it was quickly buried in a shallow grave. Some months later, a group of concerned citizens dug it up and, for reasons unknown, reburied it on the mainland.

Soon snake-weeds and vines took over Watson's old house. Several years later, an old woman from across the river moved in. According to legend, she went crazy one day and tried to burn the place down. Before she died, neighbors said she used to run around the woods at night, screaming at the top of her lungs about ghostlights out over the river and spirits rising from the ground.

The Headless Horseman of the High Plains

Out of the west Texas badlands of the Rio Nueces and across the pages of Wild West lore galloped one of the most fanciful cowboys of all time—the dreaded "headless rider," a mysterious mounted specter that brought fear to the high plains during the mid-19th century.

Thousands of people over the years claimed to have seen the ghostly rider roaming the lonely ranges on a black mustang stallion with glowing red eyes. Clad in rawhide leggings and a buckskin jacket, the figure often appeared out of nowhere—sometimes during the day, but usually at night. Always alone—though occasionally accompanied by wind and lightning—it was enough to frighten the bravest gunslinger.

The most gruesome feature about the solitary specter was that he had no head, only a gaping hole atop his shoulders where his neck should have been. According to legend, the mysterious cowboy carried his decapitated head on the front of his saddle, lashed to the horn beneath a sombrero.

So many stories cropped up about the mounted phantom in the 1840s it seems likely that more than one headless cowboy stalked the high plains. Most of the sightings occurred in the area around the Rio Nueces in the southwestern part of the state, a dismal, canyon-pocked region inhabited by rattlesnakes, scorpions, and wild mustangs.

One tenderfoot who happened to meet up with the

ghastly apparition thought he was the devil, or a demon summoned from hell. The terrified westerner fired his rifle several times at the approaching rider. Even though several bullets reportedly found their mark, they seemed to "go right through" the onrushing specter. Numerous newspaper stories and campfire tales told how other people had shot at the creature, all with the same puzzling results.

Who—or what—was the uncanny creature that, impervious to bullets, rode the lonely high plains? Some local frontiersmen swore the rider was alive—an outlaw, perhaps, who donned grisly attire for the purpose of instilling terror among the population. Others say it was the ghost of a vaquero—a Mexican cowboy—whose spiritual mission was to guard the lost gold mine of the abandoned Candelaria Mission on the Rio Nueces.

A less fantastic theory proposed that the rider was a mounted scarecrow whose job was to stampede mares into exhaustion, after which they could be easily rounded up by cowboys.

The final showdown came one day when a group of ranchers, determined to solve the mystery once and for all, gathered to lie in wait for the rider at one of his favorite haunts. That afternoon, as the apprehensive gunmen crouched behind rocks and sagebrush, a powerful thunderstorm swept in from the east. For about half an hour, lightning flashed and thunder echoed across the heavens.

Without warning, the dreaded horseman suddenly appeared, galloping at a heart-stopping pace directly toward the terrified men. Not knowing what to do, the bushwhackers finally cut loose with their rifles and six-guns. When the dust and smoke had cleared, horse and rider lay sprawled in a grotesque heap only a few yards away. The men were stunned. Clearly they had not expected such an easy end to the great mystery of the high plains.

Advancing cautiously on the felled horse and rider, they soon made a startling discovery—the black stallion was nothing more than a plain horse after all, and the rider—the dreaded black rider of lore—was actually the dried-up corpse of some long-dead cowboy strapped to the saddle.

The men saw that the corpse was riddled with hundreds of bullets and other wounds from arrows and spears. Upon closer observation, they made yet another macabre find. Beneath the rotting sombrero was a small skull, shriveled from many years in the grueling western sun.

The infamous ghost rider of the Rio Nueces was nothing more than a corpse! As the knowledge slowly settled in, the men couldn't help wondering about the identity of the poor cowboy, and who was behind such a terrible scheme, and why.

As time passed, the local ranchers learned the dead man, whose name was Vidal, was a convicted horse thief who had operated throughout much of the Southwest until his untimely end. Some linked Vidal with crimes as far east as Louisiana and Mississippi.

According to reports, Vidal's free-wheeling days as a criminal abruptly ended when he made the mistake of tangling with Creed Taylor, a hardened veteran of the Mexican War. When Taylor learned Vidal had stolen a couple of his horses, he gave chase, eventually tracking him down halfway across Texas near the Rio Nueces.

After a brief shootout, Vidal was killed. Then, to make him an example of frontier justice toward rustlers, Taylor ordered one of his men—Bigfoot Wallace—to chop off Vidal's head and strap the outlaw's body to a wild stallion. As a final fitting touch, the severed head was affixed to the saddle horn beneath a large sombrero.

Bucking and kicking, the stallion galloped off into the wilds, carrying the fearsome remains of Vidal with him.

Bibliography

Adler, Bill, ed. *UFO's.* New York: Dell Publishing, 1967.

American Heritage Books. *Mysteries of the Past.* New York: American Heritage Books, 1977.

Arens, W. *The Man-Eating Myth.* New York: Oxford University Press, 1984.

Berlitz, Charles. *The Bermuda Triangle.* New York: Doubleday & Company, 1974.

Blum, John M. *The National Experience.* New York: Harcourt Brace Jovanovich, 1973.

Bolton, Herbert E., ed. *Arrendondo's Historical Proof of Spain's Title to Georgia.* Berkeley: University of California Press, 1925.

Botkin, B.A. *A Treasury of Southern Folklore.* New York: Bonanza Books, 1967.

Bray, Warwick M., and Earl H. Swanson. *The New World.* New York: E.P. Dutton, 1976.

Brawley, Benjamin. *A Social History of the American Negro.* London: Collier Books, 1970.

Bushnell, Geoffrey Sutherland. *The First Americans.* New York: McGraw-Hill, 1975.

Carter, Hodding. *Doomed Road to Empire: The Spanish Trail of Conquest.* New York: McGraw-Hill, 1963.

Ceram, C.W. *The First American.* New York: Harcourt Brave Jovanovich, 1971.

Coulter, Merton. *The Toombs Oak*. Athens, Georgia: University of Georgia Press, 1966.

Courlander, Harold. *A Treasury of Afro-American Folklore*. New York: Crown Publishers, 1976.

Crane, Verner W. *The Southern Frontier*. New York: W.W. Norton and Company, 1981.

Daniels, Jonathan. *The Devil's Backbone: The Story of the Natchez Trace*. New York: McGraw-Hill, 1962.

Davis, Nigel. *Voyages to the New World*. New York: William Morrow and Company, 1979.

Day, A. Grove. *Coronado's Quest*. Los Angeles: University of California Press, 1964.

de la Croix, Robert. *Mysteries of the Sea*. New York: John Day Co., 1965.

Del Ray, Lester. *The Mysterious Earth*. New York: Chilton Company, 1961.

de Camp, L. Sprague. *Lost Continents*. New York: Dover Publications, 1970.

Douglas, Marjorie Stoneman. *The Everglades: River of Grass*. New York: Rhinehart & Company, 1947.

Edwards, Frank. *Flying Saucers—Serious Business*. New York: Bantam Books, 1966.

Evans, Oliver. *New Orleans*. New York: MacMillan, 1959.

Fell, Barry. *America, B.C.* New York: Demeter Press, 1977.

Fishwick, Marshall W. *Virginia: A New Look at the Old Dominion*. New York: Harper & Brothers, 1959.

Foner, Eric. *America's Black Past*. New York: Harper & Row, 1970.

Gerster, Patrick, and Nicholas Cards. *Myth in American History*. Encino, California: Glencoe Press, 1977.

Goodman, Jeffrey. *American Genesis*. New York: Summit Books, 1981.

Hamilton, Charles V. *The Black Preacher in America*. New York: William Morrow & Company, 1972.

Hudson, Charles. *The Southeastern Indians*. Knoxville: University of Tennessee Press, 1976.

Jenkinson, Michael. *Beasts Beyond the Fire*. New York: E.P. Dutton, 1980.

Kirkpatrick, F.A. *The Spanish Conquistadores*. New York: World Publishing, 1971.

Kusche, Lawrence David. *The Bermuda Triangle Mystery—Solved*. New York: Harper & Row, 1975.

Lorenzen, Corale E. *Flying Saucers: The Startling Evidence of the Invasion From Outer Space*. New York: Signet Books, 1966.

Mahan, Joseph. *The Secret: America in World History Before Columbus*. Acworth, Georgia: Star Printing Co., 1985.

Meltzer, Milton, ed. *A History of the American Negro*. New York: Thomas Y. Crowell Company, 1965.

Morison, Samuel Eliot. *The European Discovery of America: the Southern Voyages*. New York: Oxford University Press, 1974.

Oates, Stephen, and Walter Lord. *Portrait of America*. Boston: Houghton Mifflin Co., 1987.

Reader's Digest. *American Folklore and Legend*. Pleasantville, New York: Reader's Digest Associates, 1978.

Reader's Digest. *Mysteries of the Unexplained*. Pleasantville, New York: Reader's Digest Books, 1977.

Reader's Digest. *Strange Stories, Amazing Facts*. Pleasantville, New York: Reader's Digest Books

Rhyne, Nancy. *More Tales of the South Carolina Low Country*. Winston-Salem: John F. Blair, 1984.

Riegel, Robert E., and Robert G. Athearn. *America Moves West.* Hinsdale, Illinois: The Dryden Press, Inc., 1971.

Roberts, W. Adolphe. *Lake Pontchartrain.* New York: Bobbs-Merrill Company, 1946.

Sanders, Ronald. *Lost Tribes and Promised Lands.* Boston: Little, Brown and Company, 1946.

Saxon, Lyle. *Fabulous New Orleans.* New Orleans: Robert L. Crager & Company, 1950.

Snow, Edward Rowe. *Astounding Tales of the Sea.* New York: Doubleday, 1965.

Snow, Edward Rowe. *Ghosts, Gales and Gold.* New York: Dodd and Meade and Company, 1972.

Snow, Edward Rowe. *Sea Disasters and Inland Catastrophes.* New York: Dodd, Mead and Company, 1980.

Stick, David. *Graveyard of the Atlantic.* Chapel Hill: University of North Carolina Press, 1952.

Styron, William. *Nat Turner: Ten Black Writers Respond.* Boston: Beacon Press, 1968.

Sweeney, James B. *A Pictorial History of Sea Monsters.* New York: Bonanza Books, 1972.

Time-Life Books. *Mystic Places.* Alexandria, Virginia: Time-Life Books, 1987.

Vaughan, Alden. *American Genesis: Captain John Smith and the Founding of Virginia.* Boston: Little, Brown & Co., 1975.

Velikovsky, Immanuel. *Earth in Upheaval.* New York: Doubleday and Company, 1955.

Walker, Hugh. *Tennessee Tales.* Nashville: Aurora Publishers, 1970.